# THE PREVAILING WOMAN

# THE PREVAILING WOMAN

## A Devotional

*A Woman's Journey Toward Overcoming, Conquering, and Prevailing*

DR. SAMANTHA WILSON MURFREE

XULON PRESS

Xulon Press
2301 Lucien Way #415
Maitland, FL 32751
407.339.4217
www.xulonpress.com

Unless otherwise indicated, Scripture quotations taken from the Holy Bible, New International Version (NIV). Copyright © 1973, 1978, 1984, 2011 by Biblica, Inc.™. Used by permission. All rights reserved.

Printed in the United States of America.

ISBN-13: 978-1-54564-471-3

# CONTENTS

# INTRODUCTION

I am going to begin with the end in mind by saying that this journey toward prevailing is a never-ending process. I had to acknowledge that at some point. It was not what I expected to be saying, but it was a prevailing truth (pun intended). The reality of it being a never-ending process (at least on this side of heaven) became apparent one day when an old emotion emerged all at once while watching a show on television, and I burst into tears. It was the painful memory of recognizing that my innocence as a child was taken from me and that every bad relationship decision I made growing up was as a direct result of what I was exposed to as a child. I recognized that at the core of getting over any experiences are the memories associated with it. No matter how minuscule the memory may be, it has the capacity to sting, even on our best days. The desire to prevail emerges when we face a multitude of life experiences that challenge us to decide how we are going to respond. We are either going to press ahead, fight back, be overwhelmed, struggle, remain stagnant, give up, allow our emotions to dictate our response, seek wise counsel, praise and thank God, trust and have faith, believe the lies of the enemy, let our circumstances rule us, or take authority over our circumstances and finally choose to be victorious and triumphant. When we decide to prevail against, prevail through, and yes, prevail over any obstacle, it is an intentional act. The choice to prevail is always a definitive moment and choice, whether we verbalize it or actively engage in a manner that suggests we are prevailing or resigning to be defeated.

## The Prevailing Woman

So, who is this prevailing woman? I pondered this question while writing this book and resolved that she was not just one woman. The prevailing woman is a conglomeration of women with unique circumstances and situations. She is not a figment of our imagination or reflection of the ideal woman, for to imagine her as ideal suggests that she is perfect, and she is not. The prevailing woman is woven out of flaws, mistakes, struggles, faith and the lack thereof, risks that reaped no rewards, good and bad decisions, strength, endurance, hope, doubt, successes and failures, persistence, perseverance, hope, pain, disappointments, joy, and enduring love. The prevailing woman has fallen multiple times, sometimes to the same old sins and traps by the enemy, but she repeatedly gets back up. Though she experiences challenges and the appearances of setbacks, she anticipates divine outcomes to every obstacle she faces. The prevailing woman anticipates victory over defeat. Failure is not her conclusion, but success is her destination. Aspects of this woman exist, breathes, and are manifested in every woman walking on the face of the earth. The prevailing woman is you; it's me and every woman who chooses to overcome, conquer, and prevail against all odds.

The prevailing woman's devotional journal is designed to help women recognize their power and capacity to prevail over and against forces, obstacles, circumstances, and/

or situations that would hinder their God-ordained purposes, mission, plans, and growth in Jesus Christ. The devotionals will encourage women to declare victory every day over some area of their life. When you experience victory, testify about it. When we testify about how God helped us overcome, that diminishes the enemy's capacity to accuse us. There is power in our testimony and not keeping "our stuff" a secret to be held over us to make us feel guilt or shame. We are victorious over the enemy when we share our stories. These devotionals are testimonies out of my own journey with God as well as lessons gleaned from others I have been blessed to know. There is something here for everyone, married, single, divorced, young, or seasoned. There are messages that will bring encouragement, challenge your faith, convict, correct, empower, give hope, wisdom, and most of all, a compelling power to overcome. My prayer is that you will be blessed by these messages in the way they were intended and that they minister to you at the core of your needs. I am trusting God for each of you to believe and confidently declare along with me that you are a prevailing woman!

# DEDICATION

**This devotional book is dedicated to *all* the prevailing women in my life.**

The most important prevailing woman of all is my mother, Mrs. Earnestine Braxton. I have watched you overcome, conquer, and prevail too many times to name. I am thankful for your strength, courage, and love.

To my dear friend and inspiration, Deirdre A. Nixon. You were with me at a women's conference when God impressed upon my heart to write a devotional book. You are still prevailing! Praise God for your life.

# ACKNOWLEDGMENTS

I want to acknowledge God the Father, Jesus Christ the Son, and the Holy Spirit for giving me the ability, strength, and courage to finish what was put in my heart to do all those years ago. Your word is so true; "Being confident in this, that he who began a good work in you will carry it on to completion until the day of Christ" (Phil. 1:16). I want to express enormous gratitude, appreciation, and love for having a husband who supports me no matter what. He is simply the best, and I am thankful to have Joshua W. Murfree Jr. on my side. He has sacrificed the most during this journey. I also want to recognize my second mom, Mrs. Joyce Ann Robinson (Mama Joyce aka "Miss Ann"), the best stepmother in the world. She has loved me unconditionally since the first day we met. No one would know that she didn't give birth to me unless we told them. Her demonstration of what it means to prevail has not gone unnoticed.

I have been fortunate and blessed to live in a lot of places. As a result, I have developed relationships and extended family everywhere. I have a lot of authentic relationships with women I have grown to love as sisters. I have older women who have adopted me as their "daughter." It would be an oversight on my part to try and name everyone and risk forgetting someone. I simply say this to all my circle of sisters and all my adopted moms, thank you for the love and support you have shown me over the years. I have gleaned wisdom and encouragement from you all.

Thank you to my youngest brother Jarvis Robinson and my sister in-law LaKesha Robinson, who have been a constant source of support and encouragement to me ever since they learned of my passion and vision for ministry. Thank you to my cousin Tracey Henderson, who is like the little sister I never had. She has listened to my ideas, given me feedback, worked behind the scenes, and provided encouragement through this journey. Her life has been an amazing example of perseverance and persistence in fulfilling her dreams.

Again, trying to name friends is challenging because my circles run wide and deep at every stage of my life. All are very important to me. However, when I think about this ministry assignment, only a few people have been privy to what God has been doing in me over the past few months and years. Some people have been walking with me a lot longer than others, but nonetheless, our paths crossed. With that being said, these are the prevailing friends who have been privy to God's calling on my life or who have walked alongside me and prayed for me specifically during this ministry endeavor: Shantelle Leatherwood, Cassandra Jackson, Dr. Danita Bolin, Littura W. Smith, Tina Hicks, Dr. Marian Wells-Higgins, Lakesia Toomer, Latisha Bacon, Cathryn Holt and Letitia Kelly. You have been a witness to God's hand being at work at different stages and have continued to support me. I am eternally grateful to these women.

Thank you to Pastor Greg Holt, who was the first person to read my manuscript in its entirety and gave me honest feedback on how to improve what is presented. To Pastor Carlos Kelly, thank you for your leadership and support of the ministry that God has put in me. Thank you to my former pastor Dr. Eugene Sherman, for allowing me to speak on a message in 2010, which is represented in the title of this book but has also turned into my ministry. Thank you to the prayer warriors in the Beulahland Bible Church Marriage and Relationship Ministry: Vanessa Wynn, Belinda Chaney, Bessie Brown, Dr. Tonya Moore, Vanessa Walker, Cecilia Jackson, Judy Goodwin, and Hilda Jones. These ladies are always ready to intercede regardless of who needs prayer.

I am thankful for Cassie Jacobs, Tamara Andrews, and Michele Josey, who typed for me when I simply didn't have time to do it myself. Your assistance was a tremendous help. I want to thank the young women of American Technologies and IROCREATE, LLC, Cori Fowler, Kellie Fowler, and Kailah Fowler. These young women are beautiful, talented, graceful, professional, and have a spirit of excellence. They have been a blessing and joy to work with in every capacity. I am thankful for their exquisite work.

To family, friends, and colleagues who have allowed me to weave their stories into this book, I am eternally grateful for the nuggets of wisdom I have gained from each of you.

# PREVAILING WOMAN'S DEVOTIONAL JOURNEY

I t is important to understand how to utilize this devotional book to get the most out of this experience. Each day, you will read a devotional message and then be challenged to look at your present circumstances against the backdrop of God's Word. Following each devotional, you will have a journal exercise called the Prevailing Woman's Reflection. During the journal exercises, you will reflect on your current circumstances, considering both the day ahead and your current season, and relate them to the day's devotional message and scripture. You will read, reflect, and then write out your thoughts. Each day, pray for God to speak to you through the message and His Word. Lastly, and most importantly, at the end of each devotional, pray and declare that you have prevailed in Jesus's name.

You must understand the power that exists in this experience. We have the power to speak life and death over our circumstances (Prov. 18:21). This journey is about overcoming and conquering the enemy because of the blood of the Lamb and the word of our testimony (Rev. 12:11). You are testifying to the truth of God's word concerning your life and circumstances. Second Corinthians 4:13 says, "Yet we have the same spirit of faith as he had, who wrote in scripture, 'I believed, therefore I spoke.' We also believe, therefore we also speak." We have the same faith and the same power that raised Jesus Christ from the dead! Ladies, we will use our faith in Jesus and power of the Holy Spirit to speak to every circumstance we encounter on this journey toward prevailing. When we speak God's word over our life, He promises to fulfill His Word on our behalf.

## Scriptural Reference: 1 Thessalonians 5:11

*"Therefore encourage one another and
build each other up, just as in fact
you are doing."*

# HELLO, BEAUTIFUL!

"Hello, beautiful!" yes, you. You are beautiful, just in case you have not heard it in a while or no one has said it to you today. Perhaps you are not accustomed to having your outer beauty affirmed. To be honest, affirmation of our outer beauty may not be common today. Generally, people comment on our clothes, jewelry, hairstyle, shoes, or handbags, and that's all great. It certainly serves to encourage us, because we need it sometimes.

Several of my friends and I greet each other with, "Hello, beautiful!" We greet each other in person or send each other text messages with this statement. I say this to other women I meet as a term of endearment. Yes, it affirms our outer beauty, but it also builds our self-esteem and confidence. It serves as motivation and encouragement, yet it is clearly deeper than external qualities. Because my friends and I know each other, we affirm the beauty within each of us as women of God. We build each other up.

There are many stereotypes that tell us what a beautiful woman looks like on the outside, and we may believe we are not beautiful if we do not fit those stereotypes. Then, if we don't fit into the vast array of stereotypes, we have reality television and many other shows across a variety of networks that showcase negative and catty images of women, while casting them as beautiful. We do not see a lot of graceful, kind, loving, and tenderhearted women, unless it is a family-oriented television station or show. However, one night during a commercial break, an actress said, "We don't tear each other down as women." I immediately agreed with her.

Ladies, we should not tear each other down under any circumstance. We may not agree on everything (and we shouldn't), but we should always seek to live in harmony with our fellow sisters in Christ, all of them. If we, by chance, meet someone who may not have come into the saving knowledge of Jesus Christ, how we respond to them could make a difference in leading them to Jesus. We should build each other up through encouragement, showing kindness, and demonstrating love. First Thessalonians 5:11 says, "Therefore encourage one another and build each other up, just as in fact you are doing."

When our actions and words build each other, we value others above ourselves (Phil. 2:3). Calling another woman beautiful does not take away from your beauty. If Christ Jesus lives in your heart, you have a double portion of beauty; you are beautiful on the inside because of His Spirit living in you.

The next time you run into an old or current friend, greet them like this: "Hello, beautiful!" It will surely bless them.

## Prevailing in Building Up Other Women

*Therefore encourage one another and build each other up,*
*just as in fact you are doing.*

*–1 Thessalonians 5:11*

## Reflect on how you can prevail in this area of your life.

_____

_____

_____

_____

_____

_____

_____

_____

_____

_____

_____

_____

Prayer: Dear God, may I develop a heart for building up my fellow sisters, regardless of whether I know them or am just meeting them. Help me to encourage other women and show them the love of Christ. May I look not to my own interests but to the interests of others, just like Jesus did.

**I am prevailing in building up other women,**
**in Jesus's name. Amen!**

## Scriptural Reference: Matthew 15:21-28

*Leaving that place, Jesus withdrew to the region of Tyre and Sidon. A Canaanite woman from that vicinity came to him, crying out, "Lord, Son of David, have mercy on me! My daughter is demon-possessed and suffering terribly." Jesus did not answer a word. So his disciples came to him and urged him, "Send her away, for she keeps crying out after us." He answered, "I was sent only to the lost sheep of Israel." The woman came and knelt before him. "Lord, help me!" she said. He replied, "It is not right to take the children's bread and toss it to the dogs." "Yes it is, Lord," she said. "Even the dogs eat the crumbs that fall from their master's table." Then Jesus said to her, "Woman, you have great faith! Your request is granted." And her daughter was healed at that moment.*

# SHE PERSISTED AND PREVAILED

The persistence of women who have been oppressed, marginalized, discouraged, silenced, denied, or even excluded is not a new phenomenon. During my professional career, at various points I have experienced how this feels. Perhaps you know these feelings too. In spite of these experiences, we have still pressed ahead to accomplish whatever God has asked us to do. Sometimes our efforts have been out of sheer determination, other times out of inspiration, and sometimes we have been moved out of desperation.

In Matthew 5:21–28, the encounter unfolds in a moment of desperation for this woman. She needed Jesus to heal her daughter, who was demon possessed. She first pleaded with Jesus for mercy, but He did not respond to her plea. The disciples were even a deterrent as they were seemingly annoyed by her persistence. To show her belief in the power of Jesus, she kneels before the Lord and says, "Lord, help me!" (Matt. 15:25). This woman didn't let the lack of an immediate response from Jesus hinder her from pleading with Him. She didn't let the disciples' attempts to silence her or push her aside stop her from seeking a miracle from the Master. She didn't even let being compared to a pet dog obstruct her from the main objective — her daughter's need to be healed and delivered from a demonic force. In the end, Jesus declared, "Woman, you have great faith! Your request is granted" (Matt. 15:28). Jesus healed her daughter in that moment.

The lesson for us is to never give up seeking the Lord for a response to every need we have. We could easily become discouraged from persisting when we are treated with rejection, hostility, annoyance, negativity, or disregard. There will always be someone or something attempting to impede our progress or thwart our path to victory. However, the goal is to continue to seek, praise, pray, and believe by faith that it will be done. It can then be said that you persisted and prevailed!

## Prevail by Persistence

*The woman came and knelt before him, "Lord, help me!" she said.*

*–Matthew 15:25*

—◦❦◦—

**Reflect on how you can prevail in this area of your life.**

---

---

---

---

---

---

---

---

---

---

---

---

---

Prayer: Dear Sovereign God, may I be ever so persistent in prayer and faith to pursue You passionately. Do not allow distractions or moments of discouragement to hinder my desire to discover more of You and Your divine plans for my life. May You give me favor in places where I could be denied or even disregarded.

### I am prevailing in my persistence, in Jesus's name. Amen!

## Scriptural Reference: 1 Corinthians 10:12-13

*So, if you think you are standing firm, be careful that you don't fall! No temptation has overtaken you except what is common to mankind. And God is faithful; he will not let you be tempted beyond what you can bear. But when you are tempted, he will also provide a way out so that you can endure it.*

# YOU CAN RESIST

Over the years, I have been told (and later learned) that you should never go grocery shopping on an empty stomach, because you will crave all your favorite things and end up overspending. I am sure this is real for many of us. During certain times of the month (ladies, you understand what I am saying), some of us crave carbohydrates, chocolate, salt, ice cream, sweets, and whatever else our minds can conceive leading up to that time of the month. It varies for us all, but the craving is real and can be overwhelming.

The lesson is that we should never go into an environment where we are more susceptible to go beyond our established boundaries. Food and people have some things in common; both have specific ingredients that make up their compositions. The biggest commonality is that God is Creator of both. We have power over food because we choose what to eat and when to eat it. Food does not control us, but we act like it does when those hunger pangs and cravings kick in.

Now, think about people, circumstances, and situations you have encountered, or may be encountering right now in your life. Are you in control? It could be that you have allowed the food, the people (or person), circumstances, or situation to consume and overwhelm you, and you are being controlled. If so, you are not alone, and God has provided a way of escape. He never intended for us to give authority of our lives over to anyone or anything other than Jesus Christ our Savior and Lord.

It is not God's design or will for us to be overtaken by anything, regardless of the source. If you battle over indulgence, lack of boundaries, or if you have allowed yourself to be controlled by someone or something, God says you can resist, and He provides a way out. If you are in a compromising relationship that is not honoring God or your values, God says you can resist, and He provides a way out. Sisters, we can resist; we can overcome temptation. Resistance is at times the way out that God provides. The Holy Spirit compels and strengthens us to make wise choices and gives us the power to resist. Amen!

# Prevail by Resisting Temptation

*No temptation has overtaken you except what is common to mankind. And God is faithful; he will not let you be tempted beyond what you can bear. But when you are tempted, he will also provide a way out so that you can endure it.*
*–1 Corinthians 10:13*

**Reflect on how you can prevail in this area of your life.**

_____

_____

_____

_____

_____

_____

_____

_____

_____

_____

_____

Prayer: Dear Lord God, You know my weaknesses; You know the places where I need to resist. I ask for strength and power to say no to anything or anyone who hinders me from growing closer to You. Give me the power to walk away and walk after You, in Jesus's name. Amen.

**I am prevailing by resisting temptation,
in Jesus's name. Amen!**

## Scriptural Reference: Proverbs 16:9

*In their hearts humans plan their course,*
*but the Lord establishes their steps.*

# DETOURS BY DESIGN

Have you ever planned a trip, commenced to driving to your destination, and along the highway encountered a detour sign? When this happens, we have to change course, whether we want to or not. It is probably annoying that our schedule has been interrupted and plans are seemingly delayed. You could also develop some anxiety because this was not quite how you envisioned your journey and may be in unfamiliar territory.

Detours sometimes cause you to arrive later than planned. At other times, you arrive at your destination right on time. There are different types of detours. First there are divine detours, which are intentional efforts orchestrated by God to direct or redirect you toward a path you would not have chosen had He not interrupted your plans. The second is distractive detours, which are orchestrated by demonic forces designed to hinder you from accomplishing or fulfilling the plans God has established for you, or to keep you from arriving at your spiritual destiny.

Our focus here is on the divine detours. Sometimes, detours may seem familiar because it mirrors a path we have taken at other points and feels right to us. Detours are never meant for us to get comfortable, because they are a means to an end. We should be alert while taking detours. We should be listening for where God is directing us as He says, "I will instruct you and teach you in the way you should go…" (Ps. 32:8). Detours are designed for us to be safe. Yes, safe. The goal is to prevent us from encountering something hazardous on the road ahead. Sometimes, there is construction work underway and the road may be closed; at other times, there is an accident ahead or debris left over from an accident. Either way, the detour is there to protect you from unsafe encounters. Divine detours are God's way of letting us know that He sees what lies ahead and knows if we continued our route, we would not be in His will and would be subject to experience danger along the way.

Regardless of what the navigational system is saying, or what you are thinking and feeling, listen to what God is saying. We should not lean on our understanding, but acknowledge God, and He will surely make our paths straight (Prov. 3:5-6). Be aware of the type of detour you may be experiencing. Distractive detours lead to destruction and divine detours lead to destiny. We make decisions that affect the path we are on for good or bad.

In moments when detours compel us to take a new and different direction, remember God's Word, "In their hearts humans plan their course, but the LORD ESTABLISHES THEIR STEPS" (PROV. 16:9).

# Prevailing in Detours

*In their hearts humans plan their course, but the* LORD
*establishes their steps. – Proverbs 16:9*

**Reflect on how you can prevail in this area of your life.**

_____

_____

_____

_____

_____

_____

_____

_____

_____

_____

_____

_____

_____

Prayer: Lord God, thank You that You direct my path and make my ways straight. I am grateful for Your leading, directing and interrupting my life. May I be led by You and listen to Your still small voice telling me the way to walk (or drive). God, thank You for the divine detours I have had and the ones I will encounter. In Jesus's name. Amen.

**I am prevailing when faced with detours,
in Jesus's name. Amen!**

## Scriptural Reference: Ephesians 5:1-2

*Follow God's example, therefore, as dearly loved children and walk in the way of love, just as Christ loved us and gave himself up for us as a fragrant offering and sacrifice to God.*

# BEING AN EXAMPLE

There are times in life where someone pays you an extraordinary compliment that is too beautiful for words. In those moments, "Thank you" seems like such an insufficient response. A father once said to me, "I have watched my daughter working for you, and I see the 'essence of your spirit' in her." He continued with saying, "As a father, that makes me proud" and then further recounted his appreciation and admiration for being a positive influence on his daughter. Tears consumed me, because I had no idea of the impact I was having on this young woman's life. I only knew that she and her sisters were being influential in changing my future. When I reflected on this conversation more deeply, I realized that it wasn't about me. It was about Christ living in me and the example I had set through our conversations and interactions.

Being a biblical example to others is not optional; it is a requirement for all who call upon the name of the Lord. On several occasions in scripture, we are reminded to be imitators of Christ (1 Cor. 11:1; 1 Thess. 1:1:6). Our example should so reflect Jesus that others should want to know who He is. Our lifestyle should be such a reflection of who we serve that others want to emulate us. In fact, Paul specifically urges the Corinthians to imitate him as his life reflected Christ (1 Cor. 4:16). Likewise, we should be compelled to do the same thing.

The compliment I received was humbling and nothing I expected at that moment. This experience encouraged me even more so to do what it says in Matthew 5:16, "In the same way, let your light shine before others, that they may see your good deeds and glorify your Father in heaven." We never know who is watching us and what they are seeing and saying about our lives. Therefore, the example we set with our coworkers, supervisors, colleagues, and other personnel is important every day. As women, we have a chance to significantly impact the next generation of godly young women. Let us strive to "Follow God's example, therefore, as dearly loved children and walk in the way of love, just as Christ loved us and gave himself up for us as a fragrant offering and sacrifice to God" (Eph. 5:1–2).

## Prevailing As a Godly Example

*Follow God's example, therefore, as dearly loved children and walk in the way of love, just as Christ loved us and gave himself up for us as a fragrant offering and sacrifice to God.*
*– Ephesians 5:1–2*

### Reflect on how you can prevail in this area of your life.

_____

_____

_____

_____

_____

_____

_____

_____

_____

_____

Prayer: Dear Holy God, I thank and praise You for the examples You have given us all throughout scripture. You have set the example for us in wisdom, love, humility, and sacrifice. Help me to display Your goodness, grace, love, and mercy to all whom I encounter today. In areas where I have failed to display Christlikeness, may I be ever vigilant to get it right from this point forward. In the wonderful name of my Savior. Amen!

**I am prevailing as a godly example,
in Jesus's name. Amen!**

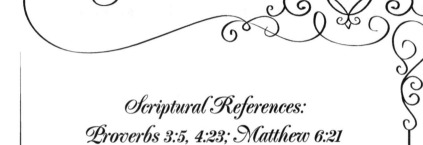

## *Scriptural References:*
## *Proverbs 3:5, 4:23; Matthew 6:21*

*Trust in the LORD with all your heart and lean
not on your own understanding (Prov. 3:5).*

*Above all else, guard your heart, for everything
you do flows from it (Prov. 4:23).*

*For where your treasure is, there your heart will be also
(Matt. 6:21).*

# DO YOU KNOW
# WHERE YOU ARE?

My husband wanted breakfast one morning while in route to work. He stopped at a local fast-food restaurant and ordered an Egg White Delight, which is sold at McDonalds. He placed his order with confidence, and then the cashier asked, "Are you sure that is what you want?"

"Yes," he replied and asked for hash browns too.

"Sir, do you know where you are?"

He explained to her that he always orders this meal.

She then said, "You are at Chick-fil-A."

To hear him tell this story is hilarious, but let's consider her question from a spiritual perspective. The question she posed asked about a physical location, which was easily answered. The question I am asking today is about the location of our hearts.

The word location itself is also synonymous with the word "position." The position of our heart says a lot about our relationship with God. For instance, in Matthew 6:21 it says, "For where your treasure is, there your heart will be also." The Amplified Bible references that your heart is "your wishes, your desires; that on which your life centers."[1]

Is your heart centered on God?

In Proverbs 3:5 it says, "Trust in the Lord with all your heart and lean not to your own understanding." Who do you lean on when you need strength, guidance, or direction?

---

[1] The Amplified Bible Matthew 6:21, The Lockman Foundation, 2015.

Are you trusting God or man? Psalm 51:10 says, "Create in me a pure heart, O God, and renew a steadfast spirit within me." Our hearts simply need to be pure and clean before our God, but He is the only One who can make it that way. Proverbs 4:23 says, "Above all else, guard your heart, for everything you do flows from it." What does your heart need guarding against?

The position of our heart determines what we do, how we do it, and whether we will do it (that is, whatever God says or calls us to do). Our heart determines our actions. There is an implication that if we don't guard our hearts, we may allow negative or destructive things to flow from us.

Psalm 37:4 reads, "Take delight in the Lord, and he will give you the desires of your heart." Our actions also determine whether God will perform on our behalf. If our hearts are aligned with God, we benefit from the blessings He bestows on us. He promises to give us the desires of our hearts. If our heart reflects the character of God, then godliness flows from our mouth. Consequently, unholiness flows from our mouth if we reflect the world.

The position of our heart should be focused on the Lord, giving evidence to our confident trust in Him. Do you know where you are? Pray and ask the Lord to show you the position of your heart, especially if you sense distance from the Lord.

## Prevailing by Aligning My Heart with God

*For where your treasure is, there your heart will be also.*
*–Matthew 6:21*

## Reflect on how you can prevail in this area of your life.

_____

_____

_____

_____

_____

_____

_____

_____

_____

_____

_____

_____

_____

_____

_____

Prayer: Lord God, may the position of my heart align totally with You. May my relationship with You grow deeper as I spend more time with You.

**I am prevailing by aligning my heart with God,
in Jesus's name. Amen!**

### *Scriptural Reference: Psalm 139:13-14*

*For you created my inmost being; you knit me together in my mother's womb. I praise you because I am fearfully and wonderfully made; your works are wonderful, I know that full well.*

# INSECURITY

As I reflect upon how I have viewed myself over the years, I can see ongoing traces of insecurities. In hindsight, I had insecurities in just about every type of relationship I established from middle school all throughout high school. It was a culmination of thinking everyone else was prettier than me, had thicker and longer hair than me, lived better than me, dressed better than me, or simply were smarter than me. The list goes on. I always thought that I had to compromise to be accepted, and I did compromise often.

The reality is that as I transitioned into adulthood, the insecurities just changed. When I was younger, I didn't really worry about my weight, but now I do. I used to be able to pass for someone twenty years younger, but not so much now. I have struggled with everything from not achieving my desired career success to worrying about my hair graying and thinning. As a result, I developed insecurities about my appearance as well as my future.

The fashion and cosmetic industries have really created an answer for every insecurity we have. We can look any part. There is a serum to take away wrinkles, dark circles, and bags under your eyes. You can tan your skin, bleach your skin, and your hair if you don't like the color. We can weave, wear a wig, install clips, braid, and crotchet our hair. We can literally change our image and everything that causes us to feel insecure. Please hear me: not all of what we do is the direct result of insecurities; sometimes, it is simple convenience because we are busy, and as women, we like changing things up every now and then. However, if we are honest with ourselves, we are not always content with how God created us. We change as we grow and develop, and in many cases, we have no control of how we change due to our genetic makeup and medical history. We try to change what we cannot control, and the fact is that we will age.

God knows us all too well because He created us in His very own image. The word says, "For you created my inmost being; you knit me together in my mother's womb. I praise you because I am fearfully and wonderfully made; your works are wonderful, I know that full well" (Ps. 139:13–14). God did a wonderful work when He created us, and that alone should be our cure for insecurity.

# Prevailing over Insecurities

*For you created my inmost being; you knit me together in
my mother's womb. I praise you because I am fearfully and
wonderfully made; your works are wonderful, I know that full well.
–Psalm 139:13–14*

## Reflect on how you can prevail in this area of your life.

_____

_____

_____

_____

_____

_____

_____

_____

_____

_____

_____

Prayer: Lord God, thank You that I am made in Your image
and created in Your likeness. I am blessed beyond measure
to know that You made me fearfully and wonderfully. How
excellent is your name Lord God in all the earth! You are
truly amazing!

**I am prevailing over insecurities, in Jesus's name. Amen!**

## *Scriptural Reference: Psalm 121*

*I lift up my eyes to the mountains—where does my help come from? My help comes from the Lord, the Maker of heaven and earth. He will not let your foot slip—he who watches over you will not slumber; indeed, he who watches over Israel will neither slumber nor sleep. The Lord watches over you—the Lord is your shade at your right hand; the sun will not harm you by day, nor the moon by night. The Lord will keep you from all harm—he will watch over your life; the Lord will watch over your coming and going both now and forevermore.*

# OUR REFUGE, KEEPER, AND PROTECTOR

Over the years, I have seen my share of tragedy, but for the most part, I have been insulated from the types of tragedies that some have faced. I remember being in my first fender-bender in college; someone failed to yield and hit me from behind.

The next accident involved another car that failed to yield. It pulled out in front of me, and I hit the car head-on. These experiences have caused me to become very careful, and probably more anxious, when driving or riding in a car with others.

I have witnessed two accidents where the vehicles were in front of me and I was either one or two cars behind the accident. Each time, I thought, *What if I had been just a little bit earlier? It could have been me.* I started to think about how I was held up because of this or that.

The last accident I observed caused me to think about the blessings in delays. Sometimes, we get anxious because we are running behind or are held up by friends who are having a great conversation. I found myself being so grateful for sitting just a little longer to listen. That delay served to position me in a place of safety. The beauty is that we serve a God who protects us from dangers seen and unseen. He is our refuge!

Psalm 46:1 says, "God is our refuge and strength, an ever-present help in trouble." God protects us from all hurt, harm, and danger that we are not even aware of most of the time

(Hallelujah!). Until we encounter danger that we have been shielded from because of His grace, we cannot grasp how God has covered us. Think about your life; you have encountered sicknesses that killed other people, but by God's grace... You have had medical procedures and complications that left others dead or forever impaired in this life, but by God's grace... Psalm 121: 8 says, "The LORD will watch over your coming and going both now and forevermore." The next time you get in your car and are running late or are delayed for any reason, just think, it *could* be God's divine way of protecting you while going out or coming in. We should always be thankful that "The LORD will keep you from all harm, he will watch over your life" (Ps. 121:7).

## Prevailing by Trusting God to Protect Me

*I lift up my eyes to the mountains, where does my help come from? My help comes from the LORD, the Maker of heaven and earth. –Psalm 121:1–2*

**Reflect on how you can prevail in this area of your life.**

_____

_____

_____

_____

_____

_____

_____

_____

_____

_____

_____

Prayer: God, thank You for being my refuge, keeper, and protector. God, I would be overwhelmed if I knew all the places, people, and things You have protected me from. Thank You for not letting any weapon formed against me prosper. In Jesus's name. Amen!

**I am prevailing by trusting God to be my refuge, keeper and protector, in Jesus's name. Amen!**

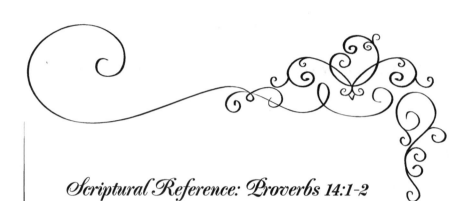

## Scriptural Reference: Proverbs 14:1-2

*The wise woman builds her house, but with her own hands the foolish one tears hers down. Whoever fears the Lord walks uprightly, but those who despise him are devious in their ways.*

# UNDER CONSTRUCTION

A dear friend, sister, and woman of extraordinary faith had this brilliant and ambitious idea for teaching character development with her summer program kids. While attempting to execute her plans, she ran into some obstacles to accomplishing it. She wanted them to build tiny houses but was told that it required getting similar approval permits required for building a regular sized house. Like any great and creative leader, she adjusted her plans and decided that the kids would get to build doll houses as well as houses out of popsicle sticks. She said the theme was "It's a construction zone" because we are under construction from the inside out. I thought to myself, what a powerful message to teach from the perspective of building a house. I immediately said, "that'll preach!" and it really does. While the aim of their lesson would be on character development, I was reminded about our spiritual development and how our character should reflect the image of Christ.

Our spiritual development has a significant impact on our spheres of influence. Consequently, we should be ever so careful how we present ourselves to family, friends, coworkers, and non-believers. Proverbs 14:1–2 says, "The wise woman builds her house, but with her own hands the foolish one tears hers down. Whoever fears the LORD WALKS UPRIGHTLY, but those who despise him are devious in their ways." Wow! We can build a house, or we can tear it down. Ladies let's just focus on us building a house for right now. So, what does building a house consist of when your aim is to reflect the image and character of Christ? The answer exists in God's word and how much time we spend reading it.

As women who identify with Jesus Christ as our foundation, God's Word is the original manual that defines, clarifies, and instructs us as to how we are to live, act, respond, and display the inner workings of a holy and transformed life, outwardly, to a dying world. God's Word repeatedly tells us to grow and gain knowledge, wisdom, and understanding (See ex. 2 Pet. 3:18; Col. 1:9–10; Eph. 4:15–16; 2 Pet. 1:5–8; Prov. 4:6–7). If we are not doing any of that, then our capacity to display spiritual maturity and Christlikeness is diminished.

Some may be wondering what spiritual maturity looks like in scripture. Characteristics that demonstrate spiritual maturity are numerous, and they include, but are not limited to: displaying love, joy, peace, patience, kindness, goodness, faithfulness, self-control (Gal. 5:22–23); delighting in God's Word (Ps. 1:1–3); and we should be imitating Christ (1 Cor. 11:1), just to name a few. The word says that a mature Christian should be like an adult who craves solid food instead of craving milk as a newborn (Heb. 5:12–14). You can test your spiritual maturity by what you are digesting. Every time we read the Bible we are establishing a stronger foundation and being built up in our faith. We are constantly under construction as we seek knowledge from the One who created us (Gen. 1:27; Col. 1:16).

# Prevailing in Spiritual Development

*The wise woman builds her house, but with her own hands the foolish one tears hers down. Whoever fears the LORD WALKS UPRIGHTLY, but those who despise him are devious in their ways.*
*–Proverbs 14:1–2*

## Reflect on how you can prevail in this area of your life.

_____

_____

_____

_____

_____

_____

_____

_____

_____

_____

_____

_____

Prayer: Lord God, may I reflect Your character in all that I do. I continue to be a work in progress that is being built up daily as I spend time in Your presence and in Your word. I am under construction. I pray that I seek You diligently to grow closer to You and learn of You.

### I am prevailing in growing spiritually, in Jesus's name. Amen!

## Scriptural Reference: Romans 8:28-31

*And we know that in all things God works for the good of those who love him, who have been called according to his purpose. For those God foreknew he also predestined to be conformed to the image of his Son, that he might be the firstborn among many brothers and sisters. And those he predestined, he also called; those he called, he also justified; those he justified, he also glorified. What, then, shall we say in response to these things? If God is for us, who can be against us?*

# REFRAMING REJECTION

W hen I was younger, I feared rejection just like most people in the world. At the point when I was old enough to date, I had these rules: break up with him before he breaks up with me; and, as soon as trouble rises, or I begin to have problems, get out of the relationship. Well, neither one of those rules ever worked out to my advantage. Like my rules about relationships, I had rules about employment opportunities: never pursue a job I don't believe I have a good chance of getting or that I am a viable and competitive candidate for the position. Even with reasonable rules for pursuing employment opportunities, it has been here that I have experienced the most rejection. Once, while waiting to hear back about a position I had interviewed for, I left town to celebrate a special birthday with a friend. The timing of the news was awful and unexpected in its form and content. The text message (*yes, text*) read, "*Samantha...have some disappointing news... [they are] moving forward with the search and you are not one of the finalists.*" I took a deep breath and let the news soak in. My emotional energy went downhill, but I knew I couldn't stay in that place, because I was out of town to celebrate. So I packed those emotions away and focused on the celebration.

I revisited those feelings the next day and the day after that too. I believed the outcome was an answer to prayer and that the entire process was a means of distracting me from what God was really calling me to do — ministry. While I was discouraged by the outcome, I could not let job rejection discourage me from areas in my life that God had affirmed. Romans 8:28 says, "And we know that in all things God works for the good of those who love him, who have been called according to his purpose." All things were working together for my good and God's glory.

Rejection does not look the same or come in the same form for everyone. Your rejection may be from family, such as never knowing one or both of your parents. Your rejection could be from a spouse who asked for a divorce, or you had to painfully decide to divorce due to infidelity. You may have just experienced a break up and were not given a reason (or reasons) why it didn't work.

Jesus experienced it all before we did. Scripture says that "He was despised and rejected by men" (Is. 53:3). Jesus was around His own people, and the Bible says, "His own people did not receive him" (Jn. 1:11). The Savior of the world was rejected, and He overcame death, conquered the grave, and prevailed in achieving salvation for us all. God ordained the outcome, which further affirms, "If God is for us, who can be against us?" (Rom. 8:31). Rejection can turn out to be a blessing and catapult your life to levels you never imagined. Rejection, though it hurts, saves us from being in places we are not destined to go and in spaces with people or in circumstances that God did not intend for us to connect with or ever get to know. Rejection never hindered God's plan for Jesus, and it should never hinder God's plan for us. Amen!

## Prevailing by Reframing Rejection

*And we know that in all things God works for the good of those who love him, who have been called according to his purpose.... What, then, shall we say in response to these things? If God is for us, who can be against us? – Romans 8:28, 31*

**Reflect on how you can prevail in this area of your life.**

_____

_____

_____

_____

_____

_____

_____

_____

_____

_____

_____

_____

Prayer: God, rejection hurts from anyone and in any form. However, You knew it would and therefore gave us the ultimate example. We have a Savior who still fulfilled His purpose despite rejection. God, may I be compelled to move forward in You even if I am rejected by man.

**I am prevailing by reframing rejection,
in Jesus's name. Amen!**

## Scriptural Reference: Luke 7:37-39

*A woman in that town who lived a sinful life learned that Jesus was eating at the Pharisee's house, so she came there with an alabaster jar of perfume. As she stood behind him at his feet weeping, she began to wet his feet with her tears. Then she wiped them with her hair, kissed them and poured perfume on them. When the Pharisee who had invited him saw this, he said to himself, "If this man were a prophet, he would know who is touching him and what kind of woman she is—that she is a sinner."*

# THE MAGNITUDE
# OF HER TEARS

I have read the account of the woman with the alabaster jar many times. It is a favorite of mine to read and ponder. Once though, as I read it, I thought about the situation differently. I considered many of this story's details. Apparently, this woman's reputation proceeded her, in that Simon the Pharisee said Jesus would know "what kind of woman she is — that she is a sinner" (Lk. 7:39). How did Simon know she was a sinner? I imagined that her counterparts in sin talked openly about her. Today, we call this talk gossip, or we might say Simon heard it from the "street committee."

Then, the next question I considered and its answer really surprised me: How many tears did she shed to wash Jesus's feet? I imagined *a lot*. Here was an act of humility, and an unmatched display of love and submission to Jesus. I have no answer to the right volume of tears it took to wash the Savior's feet; however, it was enough that she wiped them off with her hair. The entire scene demonstrates her brokenness and her literally laying it all at the feet of Jesus. Isn't this just beautiful?

Did the magnitude of her tears match the magnitude of her sins? Well, the answer is simple; it's irrelevant. Jesus pointed out that her "many sins have been forgiven — as her great love has shown..." (Lk. 7:47). Jesus recognized her repentant heart, her remorsefulness over her sins, and said to the woman, "Your faith has saved you; go in peace" (Lk.

7:50). When Jesus told her to "go in peace," He was saying be free from the distress experienced because of sin. That alone should produce a shout. No more guilt and shame. What relief He gave to her. He gives the same relief to you and me.

Scripture says that "all" have sinned (Rom. 3:23). Our sins are accompanied by ugly past lives, mine being one of them, and Jesus did for us what He did for this woman—He forgave us. Many women have been given many reasons to shed tears. We have cried over broken hearts, broken relationships, finances, health crises, and job losses. There are tears over guilt, shame, regret, fear, and even unforgiveness. The list goes on and on. The bottom line is this, when you need a breakthrough, or you want to break out of something, you will go wherever and whenever to receive what you need from the Lord. You will notice how the Pharisee served as a negative voice in this scene. The woman showed up at *his* house because she heard Jesus was there (*Had she been there before? I don't know.*). Nonetheless, she was bold in her pursuit and did not allow the location of Jesus to be a hindrance or the voice of judgement and hypocrisy keep her from kissing the feet of her Savior.

Here is the lesson: never let anyone or anything keep you from pursuing redemption and restoration from your sins. My hope is that you have appropriately grieved over your past sins (and present ones too) and sought Jesus as your source of relief, peace, and mercy. Regardless of the magnitude of your sins or the many tears you have shed, it can never surpass the omnipotent power of Jesus to save, heal, cleanse, and forgive.

# Prevailing by Receiving Forgiveness

*A woman in that town who lived a sinful life learned that Jesus was eating at the Pharisee's house, so she came there with an alabaster jar of perfume. As she stood behind him at his feet weeping, she began to wet his feet with her tears. Then she wiped them with her hair, kissed them and poured perfume on them.*
*–Luke 7:37–38*

—⚜—

**Reflect on how you can prevail in this area of your life.**

_____

_____

_____

_____

_____

_____

_____

_____

Prayer: Lord God, it is sweet to know that I can cry out to You and You will hear my cries. My tears are not wasted, and You comfort me in the process. God, thank You that I can go in peace and not be distressed over my sins because You have forgiven me. May I be like the woman with the alabaster jar and leave it all at the feet of Jesus.

**I am prevailing by receiving Your forgiveness,
in Jesus's name. Amen!**

## Scriptural Reference: John 14:1

*Do not let your heart be troubled.*
*You believe in God;*
*believe also in me.*

# HER HEART IS
# NOT TROUBLED

The first time I heard the word ablation was in the gym while walking around the track with a dear colleague who had become a great workout partner. Admittedly, I was ignorant of the word, its definition, or need in a person's life. However, I knew something was going on with my friend because we were moving rather slowly, which was the total opposite of all the other days that we met at the gym. Ablation is defined as "surgical removal" or "removal of a part…by melting or vaporization."[2] She began to shed some light as to why she was "off" on this day. She shared that she had a heart condition all her life and now her cardiologist was recommending that she have this surgical procedure on her heart. Reflecting on that day, she seemed scared, anxious, uncertain, and undecided. Though she explained what it meant, I was still limited in my understanding, but knew enough to know that it was serious. All her emotions on that day were justifiable and made sense to me as an outsider looking in.

Ironically, the Lord would connect me with another friend who used that same word, except this time it wasn't foreign to me, though I still could not explain it well. The circumstances were similar, my friend's cardiologist was also recommending that she have this procedure. Both women were

---

[2] Webster's Ninth New Collegiate Dictionary, "ablation," (Springfield, MA, 1998), 45.

faced with making life-changing health decisions regarding a heart condition. One woman chose to have the procedure, which was a success, praise God, and the other woman chose not to do so, and she is doing very well and is active as ever.

Now here is the exciting part for me. When I look at both of their lives, the issues with their hearts never stopped them from living fully engaged and vibrant lives. These women are ten years apart in age. They both are married and were blessed to each bring two children in the world. They pursued their education. They serve in their local church and volunteer in their local community. While any condition of the heart is serious and comes with a treatment regimen, they have lived like it was seemingly no trouble. One friend described it as a "defect" in her heart. My response to her was that you delivered two babies with this defect. As far as I can see, these women are examples of what a miracle looks like. Their journeys demonstrate God's faithfulness, His covering, protection, healing, and blessings. They "live by faith, not by sight" (2 Cor. 5:7). They do not live life beneath their potential or in fear of the what-ifs. While I am sure they asked all the appropriate questions, it is clear to me that the risks were worth the reward.

John 14:1 was a source of comfort and encouragement for one friend and was certainly fitting for the occasion, "Do not let your heart be troubled. You believe in God; believe also in me." These are the very words Jesus used to comfort His disciples. I say to you, prevailing woman, whatever problems you may be facing, whatever is burdening your heart today, let not your heart be troubled, but confidently trust in God to bring you through.

## Prevailing by Not Allowing My Heart to Be Troubled

*Do not let your heart be troubled (afraid, cowardly). Believe [confidently] in God and trust in Him, [have faith, hold on to it, rely on it, keep going and] believe also in Me. – John 14:1*

## Reflect on how you can prevail in this area of your life.

_____

_____

_____

_____

_____

_____

_____

_____

_____

_____

_____

_____

Prayer: Dear Father God, we can believe confidently in You even when our hearts are troubled by the cares of this world. Help us to leave our troubles with You. You will keep us in perfect peace as we keep our minds on You.

**I am prevailing by leaving my troubles in God's hands, in Jesus's name. Amen!**

## Scriptural Reference: Isaiah 32:9-11

*You women who are so complacent, rise up and listen to me; you daughters who feel secure, hear what I have to say! In little more than a year you who feel secure will tremble; the grape harvest will fail, and the harvest of fruit will not come. Tremble, you complacent women; shudder, you daughters who feel secure! Strip off your fine clothes and wrap yourselves in rags.*

# DON'T GET COMFORTABLE

P erhaps at least once in your life, you have heard someone
say the following phrases: "I just want to live comfort-
ably"; "Get comfortable with who you are"; "I am in my comfort zone"; "You need to get outside your comfort zone"; or
"Be comfortable with the skin you are in." The word comfortable can have both negative and positive connotations. One
Saturday morning while driving to meet a friend, I got this
word: "Don't get comfortable in a place where you know, and
most importantly, God knows that you are uncomfortable,
and your circumstances are causing you discomfort." I pondered what this meant and realized that comfortable in this
context was about being complacent or getting too relaxed.

In Isaiah 32:9-11, the chapter is focusing on the second
coming of Christ, while also revealing the destruction that
looms before He comes. The women of Judah did not take
the prophecy seriously. Instead of taking heed to the warnings, they continued to live life as if danger was not imminent.
They made no lifestyle changes, when the circumstances of
that day warranted significant changes. It was time to labor
in prayer to God. The women of Judah (like many of us) had
become complacent and were disregarding signs presented
during this time.

Not a lot has changed, has it? We all are guilty of ignoring
signs given to us when we know we need to make changes.
We can be our own worst enemy with a plethora of excuses we
make to justify our behavior. Staying how we are and where
we are, is always easier (so we think). We deceive ourselves

into believing that we are in a good place when we know we are in a bad place. Sometimes we stay in jobs too long, relationships too long, or make excuses to put off acquiring more skills to enhance our quality of life. We become content with complaining about others instead of complimenting one another. I have seen people choose a life of poverty over a life of progress and possibilities. Sometimes, people choose pain over joy. We overindulge and remain in all sorts of things, all in the name of comfort. We have comfort food, guilty pleasures, retail therapy, and whatever else we can think of to help us feel comfortable with our situations.

Some of us have been comfortable for a while, and it's time to get uncomfortable. Stop being complacent, and make the necessary lifestyle changes. If you know you are comfortable in a place or in any situation that does not honor God, whether it is physical, spiritual, financial, relational, emotional, or vocationally — take heed! Labor in prayer, and watch God move. Check your comfort levels.

## Prevailing against Being Comfortable

*You women who are so complacent, rise up and listen to me; you daughters who feel secure, hear what I have to say! –Isaiah 32:9*

## Reflect on how you can prevail in this area of your life.

_____

_____

_____

_____

_____

_____

_____

_____

_____

_____

_____

Prayer: Dear Lord God, help me move from a place of comfort to a place of peace and promises ordained by You. Allow me to be uncomfortable with any situation that You are warning me to move away from. Give me the strength and power to avoid complacency in this season of my life. In the name of my Savior. Amen.

### I am prevailing over complacency, in Jesus's name. Amen!

## Scriptural References: Hebrews 4:12-16

*For the word of God is alive and active. Sharper than any double-edged sword, it penetrates even to dividing soul and spirit, joints and marrow; it judges the thoughts and attitudes of the heart. Nothing in all creation is hidden from God's sight. Everything is uncovered and laid bare before the eyes of him to whom we must give account. Therefore, since we have a great high priest who has ascended into heaven, Jesus the Son of God, let us hold firmly to the faith we profess. For we do not have a high priest who is unable to empathize with our weaknesses, but we have one who has been tempted in every way, just as we are—yet he did not sin. Let us then approach God's throne of grace with confidence, so that we may receive mercy and find grace to help us in our time of need.*

# HIDDEN IMPERFECTIONS

Have you ever seen someone and thought to yourself, *that person is well put together*? It could have been a stranger or someone you know. The person could have had on a nice outfit, or had a beautiful hairstyle, nice jewelry, etc. Regardless of the external components that led you to think that this person "has it going on," you are seeing them from the outside only. You have no clue what is going on beneath the surface. You have no concept of all the hidden flaws that are being masked by all the external components covering them. You don't know that the outfit is being held together with a safety pin underneath or that there is a huge snag in their hosiery or there is a hole in the blouse that's being covered by the jacket. You also don't know the wounds that are being covered up by a pretty smile and a stylish outfit or that she maxed her credit card just to get it. You just don't know what is being covered up.

Many of us are guilty of using outerwear to cover up our lack of inner-care. I was faced with my own self-evaluation. Like many women, I have been the chick who thought a pretty outfit would make up for the pain I felt and unwisely overextended myself financially to do it. I have also thought that no one would know what was going on inside of me as long as I could "grin and bear it." We cover up flaws and imperfections to protect ourselves and to project a certain image. We protect ourselves from criticism. We want to appear to be positive and void of having problems. This approach can only last for so long before we have to come to terms with the reality of our situation or God exposes the flaws we are desperately trying to cover.

God calls us to perfection because He is perfect (Mat. 5:48); however, the reality is that we are fallible human beings. We have weaknesses and flaws that God sees in us each day. There is no hiding from God. Hebrews 4:13 says, "Nothing in all creation is hidden from God's sight. Everything is uncovered and laid bare before the eyes of him to whom we must give account." Looking at the outside is common and even natural for us to do, but God does not look on the outside to judge our appearance, He searches, examines, and tests our heart (Jer. 17:10). As a result, He knows all our flaws.

Here is the blessed assurance we have when God looks at our heart, He knows exactly how we feel and sympathizes with us (Heb. 4:15). We are free to be transparent in Christ. The word of the Lord says, "Let us then approach God's throne of grace with confidence, so that we may receive mercy and find grace to help us in our time of need" (Heb. 4:16). God sees our imperfections and loves us despite them. It is my prayer that you would use this moment to release all that you have been covering up and be set free to live your life without being bound.

## Prevailing Over All That Is Hidden

*For the word of God is alive and active. Sharper than any double-edged sword, it penetrates even to dividing soul and spirit, joints and marrow; it judges the thoughts and attitudes of the heart. Nothing in all creation is hidden from God's sight. Everything is uncovered and laid bare before the eyes of him to whom we must give account. – Hebrews 4:12-13*

**Reflect on how you can prevail in this area of your life.**

_____

_____

_____

_____

_____

_____

_____

_____

_____

_____

Prayer: Holy Father, break the chains that cause me to believe that I must cover up my flaws and pretend to be someone other than who You created me to be. Deliver me from my hidden imperfections. Set me free in Jesus's name. Amen.

**I am prevailing over my hidden imperfections, in Jesus's name. Amen!**

## Scriptural Reference: 1 Samuel 1:6-18

*Because the LORD had closed Hannah's womb, her rival kept provoking her in order to irritate her. This went on year after year. Whenever Hannah went up to the house of the LORD, her rival provoked her till she wept and would not eat. Her husband Elkanah would say to her, "Hannah, why are you weeping? Why don't you eat? Why are you downhearted? Don't I mean more to you than ten sons?" Once when they had finished eating and drinking in Shiloh, Hannah stood up. Now Eli the priest was sitting on his chair by the doorpost of the LORD's house. In her deep anguish Hannah prayed to the LORD, weeping bitterly. And she made a vow, saying, "LORD Almighty, if you will only look on your servant's misery and remember me, and not forget your servant but give her a son, then I will give him to the LORD for all the days of his life, and no razor will ever be used on his head."*

*As she kept on praying to the LORD, Eli observed her mouth. Hannah was praying in her heart, and her lips were moving but her voice was not heard. Eli thought she was drunk and said to her, "How long are you going to stay drunk? Put away your wine." "Not so, my lord," Hannah replied, "I am a woman who is deeply troubled. I have not been drinking wine or beer; I was pouring out my soul to the LORD. Do not take your servant for a wicked woman; I have been praying here out of my great anguish and grief." Eli answered, "Go in peace, and may the God of Israel grant you what you have asked of him." She said, "May your servant find favor in your eyes." Then she went her way and ate something, and her face was no longer downcast.*

# THE MISSED CARRIAGE

When I first got married, I automatically assumed that one day I would be a mother, but I didn't want that to immediately happen. However, after a year of marriage, my maternal desires intensified, so we naturally started planning. As time passed and nothing happened, I got worried and consulted with my doctor but still was unable to have a child. Through many months and years of disappointment and no explanation, I was utterly discouraged. This experience was a private pain that few people knew about or could understand unless they had experienced it. It was devastating for me to say the least. For some reading this, it is not your womb that's been closed, but God closed the door in an area of your life that you thought should have been open. In a sense, you are in a barren place where you have been unable to produce. You are unfertile in all your attempts.

My story doesn't end like Hannah's story, nor did I experience the provoking of another woman as Hannah did from Peninnah (1 Sam. 1:6) due to her being barren. I made a promise and choice that I would be happy for every woman I encountered who was pregnant and that I would not be bitter. I kept that promise and celebrated the blessing of new life. In all honesty, I never thought I would recover from the pain and sadness I felt from this journey or the disappointment I felt toward God. I truly believed that He would bless me to have a baby of my own, but to date, He has chosen not to do so. Over time the Lord healed my heart, and I am at peace with my circumstances and am very blessed. I have learned to be content (Phil 4:11) and know that God is more than able!

During the time of Hannah, the customs of her day dictated a lot of things, such as producing a son, as the firstborn son would inherit certain birthrights and inherit his father's leadership and authority within the family. Things were much harder then. Hannah is living proof that you can miss what you never carried. She mourned the opportunity to have a child in a culture that thought less of you if you couldn't. Scripture says that the Lord closed her womb for reasons we don't understand, and then He opened her womb for reasons I do now think we understand.

Hannah found favor with the Lord after pouring her heart out to God, so much so she was perceived to be drunk (1 Sam. 1:13). God was moved by her anguish. I imagined this was not the first time she pleaded with God over her desire to have a baby. In my mind, Hannah pleaded and cried out to the Lord every time Peninnah was pregnant and pleaded even more after she was provoked and taunted by Peninnah. But this time was different; God acted on her behalf. God did not bless her only because she was sorrowful in her spirit and made a promise to give the child back to Him. The Lord blessed her because of His plan and purpose for her life and her future son. Hannah was divinely used to bring forth the youngest prophet in the world, Samuel.

The lesson for us is to continue to trust God even in seasons of barrenness. We are to seek out God's plan and purpose for our lives. God could be preserving you for something greater. Lastly, if you make a promise to God, keep it, because He fulfills His promises to us. Most importantly, His promises to us are designed to fulfill His plans and purposes through and for us.

## Prevailing in a Barren Season

*And she made a vow, saying, "Lord Almighty, if you will only look on your servant's misery and remember me, and not forget your servant but give her a son, then I will give him to the Lord for all the days of his life, and no razor will ever be used on his head.*
*–1 Samuel 1:11*

**Reflect on how you can prevail in this area of your life.**

_____

_____

_____

_____

_____

_____

_____

_____

_____

_____

Prayer: Dear Lord God, You have divine purposes even in seasons of barrenness. How I thank You that You are the Sovereign Lord who can do exceedingly and abundantly more than we can ever ask or think. In Jesus's name. Amen.

**I am prevailing, even in seasons of barrenness, in Jesus's name. Amen!**

*Scriptural Reference: Colossians 4:6*

*Let your conversation be always full of grace, seasoned with salt, so that you may know how to answer everyone.*

# WORDS VERSUS SILENCE

How many times in your life have you said something you wished you could take back? And how many times have you felt justified in whatever it was that you said? You know the self-gratification that comes from believing it was utterly necessary for the statement to be made and expressed just as you said it, for fear of losing the desired impact. Well, I have been there a time or two, and I imagine that on occasion you have been there as well (at least once). This happened to me during a parking lot incident with a complete stranger some years ago. More than enough had been uttered to me, and in return, I said more than enough right back. Needless to say, it escalated! Sometimes, we are guilty of giving harsh responses to the ones we love as well as the ones we would rather disregard. We unwisely, and sometimes unashamedly, choose to utter words to and at people to relieve any pent-up anxiety or frustration. We do not always consider what our words do to the receiver.

If you have dished out a few words here and there, you have probably taken in a few words from others and may be quite familiar with how it feels to be "told off." The wrong choice of words simply hurt. Words can crush and wound a person's spirit, which leads to discouragement. Scripture says, "A good man brings good things out of the good stored up in his heart, and an evil man brings evil things out of the evil stored up in his heart. For the mouth speaks what the heart is full of" (Lk. 6:45). We can appear mean, arrogant, selfish, and insensitive to the feelings of other people if the wrong thing comes forth from our mouth. Speaking "the truth in love" has become distorted by people saying what's in their head and hearts, which does not reflect the love we profess to have for others. Believers in Jesus Christ should know better, but we are sometimes the worst offenders. Proverbs 13:3 says, "Those who guard their lips preserve their lives, but those who speak rashly will come to ruin." Real Christ-likeness calls each of us to a higher standard of living and responding, so as not to ruin ourselves.

The golden rule of doing "to others as you would have them do to you" (Lk 6:31) seems so appropriate as the ideal way to approach communication. If we reflect upon how certain forms of communication have caused us to feel, which does include facial expressions, we should certainly pause before we express any perceived, justifiable commentary to another person. Sometimes, it is just more honorable to be silent. In the moments we choose to be silent, we have exhibited the humility of Christ. Recall when Jesus chose to be silent before his accusers (Lk. 23:9–10). He could have pleaded His case fiercely and would have been justified in His efforts, but He chose to be silent. Truth prevailed regardless, and God's will was still accomplished. Jesus humbled himself even unto death. We must discern when to speak and when to be silent. And when we prayerfully and humbly choose not to be silent, our words must be full of grace. Colossians 4:6 says, "Let your conversation be always full of grace, seasoned with salt, so that you may know how to answer everyone."

## Prevailing in Graceful Communication

*Let your conversation be always full of grace, seasoned with salt, so that you may know how to answer everyone.* – Colossians 4:6

### Reflect on how you can prevail in this area of your life.

Prayer: Dear God, let my words honor You and be a blessing to others. I know that my tongue has the power to praise and curse, so help me to choose words that are full of grace. God, guide me in discerning when to speak and when to remain silent. For Your glory. Amen.

**I am prevailing by speaking words that are full of grace, in Jesus's name. Amen!**

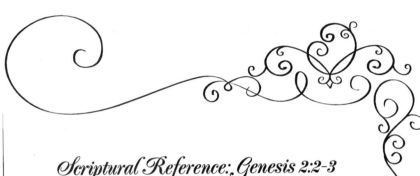

## *Scriptural Reference: Genesis 2:2-3*

*By the seventh day God had finished the work he had been doing; so on the seventh day he rested from all his work. Then God blessed the seventh day and made it holy, because on it he rested from all the work of creating that he had done.*

# THE ENEMY OF SLEEP DEPRIVATION

The conversation went something like this: "Thank you, honey, for encouraging me to get some rest." He replied, "That's how you beat the enemy." I asked for clarity; "That's how you beat the enemy of what?" He said, "The enemy of lack of sleep." I then said, "The enemy of sleep deprivation." He said, "That sounds good too." Rest is the antidote for lack of rest. Oh, how we need rest, yet spend most of our time being active. Rest is biblically defined in different ways depending upon the context. It is synonymous with ceasing, relaxation, cessation, repose, and refreshment.

In Mark 6: 30–31, "The apostles gathered around Jesus and reported to him all they had done and taught. Then, because so many people were coming and going that they did not even have a chance to eat, he said to them, 'Come with me by yourselves to a quiet place and get some rest.'" Rest is not just a problem we deal with today because we have such busy lives, clearly back in Jesus's day, getting rest was a challenge while they were constantly on the move and serving others without all the conveniences and devices that are at our disposal today.

Being sleep deprived robs us of the key ingredients we need to run with endurance the race marked out for us (Heb. 12:1). We lack energy, strength, clarity, peace of mind, and the ability to focus. Therefore, we suffer spiritually, physically, mentally, and emotionally. My ability to hear from God and discern God's will is affected. I am easily irritated and can be very impatient with my spouse, family, friends, colleagues, and even strangers. Sleep deprivation can lead to missing out on an encounter with God. It leads to delayed productivity at work, and then you just feel miserable overall. Lack of rest is also an opportunity for the devil to distract us, steal our joy, and even confuse us. Ladies, we need rest like we need food and water. Rest restores, rejuvenates, and refreshes us. We gain strength when we rest. The enemy wants us to be weak and vulnerable. He relishes in moments when we are not on our "A-game." We are way more susceptible to mistakes, which has a ripple effect depending on where we made the mistake and how significant of a mistake it was.

We are called to rest. Rest is mentioned as both a verb and noun in scripture. When rest is mentioned in scripture, it is usually preceded by or followed by the Lord's reasoning for why we should rest. We should rest because God rested from His works and called us to rest (Gen. 2:2–3, Gen. 4:9–11, Ex. 23:12). God promised He would give rest (Ex. 33:14); we need rest to eat and to escape from crowded spaces (Mk. 6:31). We need rest from working so hard to provide for our families (Ps. 127:2). We need rest for peace of mind (Ps. 4:8; Is. 26:3). Resting is an act of obedience to the Lord (Ex. 20:8–10). We are strengthened when we rest (Is. 40:29–31). We are refreshed and restored when we rest (Ps. 23:2–3).

Let us prevail over sleep deprivation by pursuing rest for our mind, body, and soul.

## Prevailing over Sleep Deprivation

*By the seventh day God had finished the work he had been doing; so on the seventh day he rested from all his work. Then God blessed the seventh day and made it holy, because on it he rested from all the work of creating that he had done.* – Genesis 2:2–3

**Reflect on how you can prevail in this area of your life.**

_____

_____

_____

_____

_____

_____

_____

_____

_____

_____

_____

_____

_____

Prayer: Lord God, may we find rest in You and from You in every aspect of our lives. May we intentionally slow down from all that occupies our time. Thank You that You are the Creator of rest for our mind, body, spirit, and soul.

**I am prevailing over sleep deprivation,
in Jesus's name. Amen!**

## *Scriptural Reference: Galatians 5: 1, 13-16*

*It is for freedom that Christ has set us free. Stand firm, then, and do not let yourselves be burdened again by a yoke of slavery... You, my brothers and sisters, were called to be free. But do not use your freedom to indulge the flesh; rather, serve one another humbly in love. For the entire law is fulfilled in keeping this one command: "Love your neighbor as yourself." If you bite and devour each other, watch out or you will be destroyed by each other. So I say, walk by the Spirit, and you will not gratify the desires of the flesh.*

# SET FREE

Prevailing woman, I think that it is fair to say that we all have had a moment when something didn't fit, or we got stuck in something and needed help getting out. I reflected on this after an evening of girl time with friends who were trying on some clothes I was giving away. This also happens any time women go shopping together, and we underestimate our capacity to get in and out of certain types of clothes. This is further underscored by our fluctuating sizes because of weight gain or weight loss. Sometimes we put clothes on that we can't get off without the help of someone else. We need someone to zip and unzip, hook and unhook, and button and unbutton us from whatever we have put on our bodies. We may have gotten into the outfit, dress, pants, or blouse by ourselves, but we cannot manage getting out of it without a helping hand.

Pivot in your mind to a circumstance or situation that you may have found yourself in and could not get out of it. For example, you took a job for the wrong reasons, and now it is difficult to get out of it, because you can't afford to leave. It could be a bad business decision that has to run its course. You may have been betrayed by a friend, and now you need to sever those ties. Just like the relief you feel when you have taken that tight blouse, pants, or dress off your body, you feel supernatural relief when you are set free by Jesus Christ, but the feeling is much, much better. We have enormous freedom in Christ, and we should not take this for granted. John 8:36

says, "So if the Son sets you free, you will be free indeed." When we trust in Jesus Christ, we are unquestionably liberated. That sounds good until we start exercising our freedoms in ways that do not align with God. We may engage in unhealthy lifestyles, poor work ethics, creating division in your family or church, unwholesome talk, or have a bad attitude. The thought process is, *I can just ask for forgiveness.* When Jesus set us free, the Word of God instructs us to stand firm and "Do not let yourselves be burdened again by a yoke of slavery" (Gal. 5:1). This is saying do not go back to your old habits, ways, and even old people who may have served as a stronghold in your life. In other words, we should "live as free people, but do not use your freedom as a cover-up for evil..." (1 Pet. 2:16).

Our freedom in Christ is indisputable and was settled on the cross at Calvary. Romans 8:22 tells of the benefits, blessings, and rewards of being liberated. "But now that you have been set free from sin .... the benefit you reap leads to holiness, and the result is eternal life." Value your freedom as it was given to help you live a victorious life that brings honor and glory to God.

## Prevailing in Freedom

*You, my brothers and sisters, were called to be free. But do not use your freedom to indulge the flesh; rather, serve one another humbly in love. For the entire law is fulfilled in keeping this one command: "Love your neighbor as yourself." If you bite and devour each other, watch out or you will be destroyed by each other. So I say, walk by the Spirit, and you will not gratify the desires of the flesh. So I say, walk by the Spirit, and you will not gratify the desires of the flesh. – Galatians 5:13-16*

**Reflect on how you can prevail in this area of your life.**

_____

_____

_____

_____

_____

_____

_____

_____

Prayer: Heavenly Father, thank You that I am free. Thank You that You liberated me through Christ's death and resurrection from the grave. God, I pray that You deliver me from every indulgence of the flesh that does not reflect Your holiness. Set me free from any chains that have me bound. In Jesus's name, Amen.

**I am prevailing in being set free from anything that has me bound, in Jesus's name. Amen!**

## Scriptural Reference: Matthew 18:7-8

*Woe to the world because of the things that cause people to stumble! Such things must come, but woe to the person through whom they come! If your hand or your foot causes you to stumble, cut it off and throw it away. It is better for you to enter life maimed or crippled than to have two hands or two feet and be thrown into eternal fire.*

# THE BLIND SPOT

I had a scary experience on the interstate some time ago while driving home one night. I was attempting to change lanes and did not see the vehicle there already; it was in my blind spot. I swerved as if I was losing control of the vehicle. It really shook me up. I felt horrible and started apologizing to the other driver as if they could hear me from my vehicle. Of course, they couldn't hear me, and the driver did what I would have done, sped up to get out of my way. (They probably had some choice words for me as well.) I regained my composure and drove on home. So many things flooded my mind. This was not the first time I hadn't observed my surroundings and didn't see a vehicle in my blind spot. By the grace of God, each time this has happened, I have caught myself in time and pulled back into my lane. A blind spot certainly prohibits and obstructs our sight. One dictionary defined it as "an area in which one fails to exercise judgement or discrimination".[3] This is certainly applicable when it comes to not looking or seeing well before merging into another lane. Our view is obstructed due to the design of our vehicles and our failure to look and exercise caution while driving.

I wondered about the blind spots in our spiritual lives. You may be asking what kind of blind spots? We have spiritual blind spots, which are all the ways we are prevented from seeing areas that are a hindrance to God's purpose and plans for us. The spiritual blind spots come in many forms

---

[3] Ibid., 159

and serve as obstacles and barriers. For example, a spiritual blind spot could be disregarding all the red flags in an abusive relationship. Your blind spot could be trusting colleagues on your job who mean you harm. Your blind spot could be pride. For others, it could be jealousy or envy. Your view could be obstructed due to emotional issues, betrayal, gossip, and lack of trust. You could also be exercising poor judgment in your finances, such as excessive spending to get your nails done or to buy designer handbags and clothes when you cannot pay all your bills.

Blind spots can be physical (people and things), mental, emotional, and spiritual obstacles that we all face in one form or another. So, what's obstructing your view? Who is in your blind spot? Where are you failing to exercise good judgment? Lastly, are you the blind spot in someone else's life? Are you blocking someone else's view? Scriptures says, "Therefore let us stop passing judgment on one another. Instead, make up your mind not to put any stumbling block or obstacle in the way of a brother or sister" (Rom. 14:13). We can pray and ask God to help us have discernment and strength. We can also seek God for wisdom in knowing when to remove ourselves from difficult situations as well as how not to be the one who causes someone else to be in an uncomfortable situation. Check your blind spots to ensure that you are not a hindrance to other people overcoming and being delivered.

## Prevailing over Blind Spots

*Woe to the world because of the things that cause people to stumble! Such things must come, but woe to the person through whom they come! If your hand or your foot causes you to stumble, cut it off and throw it away. It is better for you to enter life maimed or crippled than to have two hands or two feet and be thrown into eternal fire. – Matthew 18:7–8*

**Reflect on how you can prevail in this area of your life.**

_____

_____

_____

_____

_____

_____

_____

_____

_____

_____

Prayer: God, I pray that I am not a blind spot in someone else's life. I pray against any blind spots attempting to infiltrate my life. Lord God, clear my path of anything that is obstructing me from experiencing more of You. For the glory of Christ, I pray. Amen.

**I am prevailing over the blind spots in my life, in Jesus's name. Amen!**

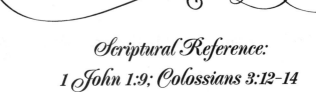

## Scriptural Reference:
## 1 John 1:9; Colossians 3:12-14

*If we confess our sins, he is faithful and just and will*
*forgive us our sins and purify us from all unrighteousness.*
*(1 Jn. 1:9)*

*Therefore, as God's chosen people, holy and dearly loved,*
*clothe yourselves with compassion, kindness, humility,*
*gentleness and patience. Bear with each other and forgive*
*one another if any of you has a grievance against someone.*
*Forgive as the Lord forgave you. And over all these virtues*
*put on love, which binds them all together in perfect unity*
*(Col. 3:12–14).*

# ABOUT FORGIVENESS

At some point, over the course of several weeks, I heard a lot about forgiveness. Usually, when I hear a word on a subject more than once or twice, it means that I really need to check myself and pay close attention to how it applies to my life. What I tend to discover is that it is something I need to do or address in some way. In this instance, I needed to address areas of forgiveness in my life. I had been harboring negative feelings due to being offended and disrespected by family members. I was not only hurt but angry. At that point, I resolved that I was done with both persons. But that only scratched the surface of my issues with forgiveness. I really had to look deeper to address unresolved feelings from past years.

I have a feeling that I am not alone with having unresolved issues with forgiveness. Not only did I need to forgive, I also needed healing. I pressed my way through the process, as painful as it was and without apologies from either person. I reconciled with family members, and God has been healing me in those other areas of my life.

Here is what I gleaned from this forgiveness journey. When you need to deal with forgiveness, start with God's word. The Bible says, "In him we have redemption through his blood, the forgiveness of sins, in accordance with the riches of God's grace" (Eph. 1:7). Then we continue on and read in 1 John 1:9 that "If we confess our sins, he is faithful and just and will forgive us our sins and purify us from all unrighteousness." These passages of scripture point to our personal need for forgiveness. However, the second point is about forgiving others. Is there someone you need to forgive or is someone asking for forgiveness? Hear God's Word, "Therefore, as God's chosen people, holy and dearly loved, clothe yourselves with compassion, kindness, humility, gentleness, and patience. Bear with each other and forgive one another if any of you has a grievance against someone. Forgive as the Lord forgave you" (Col. 3:12–13).

What I am learning is that forgiveness works in several ways: we ask for forgiveness; we receive forgiveness; we accept forgiveness; and, we give forgiveness. "For if you forgive other people when they sin against you, your heavenly Father will also forgive you. But if you do not forgive others their sins, your Father will not forgive your sins" (Matt. 6:14–15). God forgives us; we receive God's forgiveness; we forgive others; others forgive us; and, we are to forgive ourselves. We seldom do the latter or struggle to do it. The Word of God calls us to forgiveness. There is healing and restoration when we forgive. Forgiveness requires humility. Pride and arrogance are not a part of forgiveness. No one likes admitting he or she is wrong, but everyone likes to be right. The truth is that forgiveness, in any direction it is extended, makes you right with God. We are simply modeling God's Word and what He has commanded us to do.

## Prevailing in Forgiveness

*Therefore, as God's chosen people, holy and dearly loved, clothe yourselves with compassion, kindness, humility, gentleness and patience. Bear with each other and forgive one another if any of you has a grievance against someone. Forgive as the Lord forgave you. And over all these virtues put on love, which binds them all together in perfect unity. — Colossians 3:12–14*

**Reflect on how you can prevail in this area of your life.**

_____

_____

_____

_____

_____

_____

Prayer: Heavenly Father, thank You for demonstrating what forgiveness looks like by first forgiving me. I pray that I grow in my capacity to forgive others. God, I admit that some areas of forgiveness are harder than others, but I trust You to make my heart tender toward those who are more difficult to forgive. May I truly learn to forgive those who trespass against me. Lastly, Lord God, help me to also forgive myself as quickly as You forgive me of my sins. In Jesus's name, I have victory in forgiveness. Amen!

**I am prevailing in forgiving others and myself, in Jesus's name. Amen!**

## Scriptural Reference: Ephesians 2:4-6

*But because of his great love for us, God, who is rich in mercy, made us alive with Christ even when we were dead in transgressions—it is by grace you have been saved. And God raised us up with Christ and seated us with him in the heavenly realms in Christ Jesus.*

# LIVING...

O ver the past few years, I have seen a lot of people lose loved ones unexpectedly. My husband and I both have lost several loved ones that meant a lot to us. The one that stands out the most is the loss of a young lady he and I both mentored. She considered us her second set of parents and was like an adopted daughter to us. It was a devastating loss that still confounds me. In all these losses, I have pondered the life that each of these individuals lived. Were they "living abundantly" or just "living dead"? Another way of saying it is, were they spiritually alive or spiritually dead? I even questioned whether I could have done more to influence them living a more abundant life. In some cases, the answer is yes because of the relationship or connection I had.

Abundant living is the life that comes from living for Jesus Christ and bearing His fruit (Gal. 5:22-23). It is a life marked by joy and vibrancy, even amid daily challenges. It is separate from a life marked by worldliness, where the thief comes to steal, kill, and destroy (Jn. 10:10). Living dead is an oxymoron because life and death cannot coexist. However, the word of God in Revelation 3:1 says, "I know your deeds; you have a reputation of being alive, but you are dead." The living dead are individuals who are physically alive but are spiritually dead or spiritually lifeless — devoid. Those who are spiritually dead can imitate abundant life. They live according to their own standards and practice religious rituals out of cultural habit rather than having a relationship with the Savior. They have a "form of godliness but denying its power" (2 Tim. 3:5). Those who live like this are only fooling themselves, "The LORD does not look at the things people look at. People look at the outward appearance, but the Lord looks at the heart" (1 Sam. 16:7).

Those who are spiritually alive, live an authentic life. There is an intentional effort to honor God with their lifestyle; they reject pretending to be holy. Spiritually alive saints pursue living abundant lives whether on the job, at church, in relationships, or at home. We can survey ourselves, family members, and our friends and assess how we are living. People can also look at your life and determine how you are living, that is, what type of fruit you are bearing. Luke 6:43–44 says, "No good tree bears bad fruit, nor does a bad tree bear good fruit. Each tree is recognized by its own fruit…" When others witness your life, be encouraged to live as a shining and holy example of Christ's love by bearing good fruit.

Ladies, we can be a living testimony to others who need encouragement and prayer to live for God. We can share about God's mercy and grace extended to us, as well as how we were made alive in Christ.

## Prevailing in How You Live

*But because of his great love for us, God, who is rich in mercy, made us alive with Christ even when we were dead in transgressions — it is by grace you have been saved. And God raised us up with Christ and seated us with him in the heavenly realms in Christ Jesus. — Ephesians 2:4–6*

**Reflect on how you can prevail in this area of your life.**

_____

_____

_____

_____

_____

_____

_____

_____

_____

_____

_____

Prayer: God, what a joy and privilege it is to have abundant life through Jesus Christ. May I be a witness to all who are within my sphere of influence and especially those who are closest to me. In the glorious name of Jesus. Amen.

**I am prevailing in living an abundant life, in Jesus's name. Amen!**

## Scriptural Reference: Romans 7:18-24

*For I know that good itself does not dwell in me, that is, in my sinful nature. For I have the desire to do what is good, but I cannot carry it out. For I do not do the good I want to do, but the evil I do not want to do—this I keep on doing. Now if I do what I do not want to do, it is no longer I who do it, but it is sin living in me that does it. So I find this law at work: Although I want to do good, evil is right there with me. For in my inner being I delight in God's law; but I see another law at work in me, waging war against the law of my mind and making me a prisoner of the law of sin at work within me. What a wretched man I am! Who will rescue me from this body that is subject to death?*

# DOING THE RIGHT THING

One day, I decided to do absolutely nothing but rest and chill out. I had no agenda but to watch television, catch March Madness highlights, and whatever caught my eye while channel surfing. Well, the thing that arrested my attention was not wholesome at all but was very funny. I started watching a movie with some of my favorite actors. Off and on throughout the movie, I felt convicted that it was crude (Eph. 5:4), occasionally indecent, and had references of sexual innuendos. I kept watching it anyway while continuously grieving and quenching the Holy Spirit (Eph. 4:30; 1 Thess. 5:19). At that moment, the fact that it was funny outweighed the truth of God's expectation of me, which requires that I live holy as He is holy (1 Pet. 1:15–16). So, I finished watching the entire thing. (Yep, the whole thing!) Afterward, I felt ashamed and even distant from the Lord. It took a few days to recover from that experience.

I am sure that you have found yourself in a situation where you knew the right thing to do, but still chose to do the wrong thing anyway. It may not have been watching television, but it could have been unwholesome chatter, not showing kindness, managing your time at work, being impatient, yelling at your children or spouse, being a source of discouragement, not supporting a family member, friend, or colleague, or just holding a grudge and being bitter. It could be anything that you know would disappoint the heart of God.

After I repented over my actions, the Holy Spirit immediately called to mind Romans 7:18-20, which speaks about our sinful nature. God knew that we would make mistakes and occasionally choose to do the wrong thing. He planned our future and made provision for all the moments we yielded to our human nature. Paul closes out this chapter saying, "What a wretched man I am! Who will rescue me from this body that is subject to death? Thanks be to God, who delivers me through Jesus Christ our Lord!" Since we know our weaknesses and capacity to sin knowingly, why not strive to do the right thing in all the places that challenge our lifestyle of faith.

## Prevailing in Doing the Right Thing

*For I know that good itself does not dwell in me, that is, in my sinful nature. For I have the desire to do what is good, but I cannot carry it out. For I do not do the good I want to do, but the evil I do not want to do — this I keep on doing. Now if I do what I do not want to do, it is no longer I who do it, but it is sin living in me that does it.* — *Romans 7:18–20*

**Reflect on how you can prevail in this area of your life.**

_____

_____

_____

_____

_____

_____

_____

_____

_____

_____

Prayer: Almighty God, You know when I sleep and when I rise. God You also know when and where I may do the wrong thing. Guide me in making right decisions to please and bring glory to Your holy and precious name. Amen.

**I am prevailing in doing the right thing, in Jesus's name. Amen!**

## Scriptural Reference:
## 2 Corinthians 4:7-9, 15-18

*But we have this treasure in jars of clay to show that this all-surpassing power is from God and not from us. We are hard pressed on every side, but not crushed; perplexed, but not in despair; persecuted, but not abandoned; struck down, but not destroyed...All this is for your benefit, so that the grace that is reaching more and more people may cause thanksgiving to overflow to the glory of God. Therefore we do not lose heart. Though outwardly we are wasting away, yet inwardly we are being renewed day by day. For our light and momentary troubles are achieving for us an eternal glory that far outweighs them all. So we fix our eyes not on what is seen, but on what is unseen, since what is seen is temporary, but what is unseen is eternal.*

# PERPETUAL PRESSURE, PROBLEMS, AND POWER

S he had it planned in her mind how life would look. Her vision for a spouse, career, and children were not unrealistic and did not differ from what most women ideally want. The Lord God had other plans. We met over twenty years ago while we were both seeking graduate degrees, and God divinely ordained a lifetime friendship. I have grown to admire her for so many reasons, but most significantly for her capacity to persevere during hardship. Over the years I have known her; there honestly has not been a year that her life has been easy or without significant challenges. I am not exaggerating when I say it has always been something with her and her family, but they have always overcome.

As I reflect upon her life, I watched her transition from being a single woman to a wife, a mother of three children and functioning as a "nurse" to her husband, who has a chronic illness. We have cried, rejoiced, prayed, and been utterly disappointed at the course of the events that have happened over the years. From the outside looking in, it has been a litany of continuous hardship. We can easily explain some of it by the obvious, but in our human minds it is almost incomprehensible and unfathomable, let alone explainable. Through it all, regardless of how bumpy, messy, difficult, exhausting, frustrating, discouraging, and dark the numerous experiences have been, this prevailing woman has continued to pursue the Lord God during perpetual problems and hardships. Even in years where they experienced joys, there still would be some degree of pain, disappointment, or crisis. The average person would want to give up on life, but by God's power she is still pressing toward the mark of the high calling. Her entire life's testimony is an encouragement to me and so many others who know her.

I am reminded of Paul in 2 Corinthians chapter 4, where he is reflecting on the constant challenges that he has faced in his efforts to share the gospel message. He acknowledged that his journey has not been free of difficulty or without attacks from the enemy. Though he recognizes the difficulties, he also expresses victory. Paul wrote, "We are hard pressed on every side, but not crushed; perplexed, but not in despair; persecuted, but not abandoned; struck down, but not destroyed" (2 Cor. 4:8–9). Maybe your life has not been under constant pressure, but perhaps you have been perplexed and unsure how you were going to find your way out. Either way, this passage should encourage you to see the victory on the other side. Even if you have had to suffer, it did not destroy you. When we seek the Lord daily to help us through our troubles, we are renewed by His power. Because He renews us "we do not lose heart." (2 Cor. 4:16). The praise is that "our light and momentary troubles are achieving for us an eternal glory that far outweighs them all" (2 Cor. 4:17). Paul reminds us to look "not on what is seen, but on what is unseen, since what is seen is temporary, but what is unseen is eternal" (2 Cor. 4:18). Regardless of the hardships, struggles, or crises you might be facing now or in the future, the pressure of it all does not outweigh the perpetual power of Jesus Christ to carry you through, and for that alone, you ought to praise Him in advance.

# Prevailing over Pressures and Problems

*We are hard pressed on every side, but not crushed; perplexed,*
*but not in despair; persecuted, but not abandoned; struck down,*
*but not destroyed... For our light and momentary troubles are*
*achieving for us an eternal glory that far outweighs them all. So,*
*we fix our eyes not on what is seen, but on what is unseen, since*
*what is seen is temporary, but what is unseen is eternal.*
*— 2 Corinthians 4:8–9, 17–18*

**Reflect on how you can prevail in this area of your life.**

_____

_____

_____

_____

_____

_____

_____

Prayer: Dear Omnipotent and Omnipresent God, I marvel in all the ways that You confound the enemy by using even the worst of circumstances to bring glory to Yourself. You have provided so many examples of overcomers in scripture, and I delight in knowing that You can do the same things on my behalf. No hardship will overtake me, and no problem will perplex me. This is momentary and light distress passing over me. I declare this and believe the truth of Your Word. In the perpetual power of Jesus, the Christ, I pray. Amen!

**I am prevailing in trusting the perpetual power of Jesus Christ, in His name. Amen!**

*Scriptural Reference: Proverbs 19:21*

*Many are the plans in a person's heart, but it is the Lord's purpose that prevails.*

# A CALCULATED RISK

O ne evening while leaving work, I encountered a coworker who was nearing the end of his tenure as an employee. He was making a transition to pursue new endeavors. I asked him if he was excited, and he replied, "Well, it's basically a calculated risk." Because I knew him to be a man of God, I quickly responded there is no calculated risk when you trust God. He quickly agreed. This stirred up both of our spirits as we reflected on how God operates.

The phrase "a calculated risk" stayed with me all evening. It implied a lack of dependency on God, and total dependency on a set of circumstances being aligned perfectly for a person to experience a desired outcome. This is not faith. It sounded more like facts and figures. I expected my coworker to say that he was stepping out on faith! Recall Genesis 12:1: "The LORD had said to Abram, 'Go from your country, your people and your father's household to the land I will show you.'" He did as God had commanded, which was an act of faith as well as obedience. Similarly, this colleague was leaving a secure environment, that included a job with benefits, to live a life of full-time ministry. At any point, when you have no idea what the future holds, yet you keep pressing ahead, that is an act of faith.

There is nothing risky about God. We cannot calculate how things will play out, we simply trust that God will work everything in our favor as we trust Him. A faith journey is subject to take numerous unexpected turns and twists until you land in the perfect will of God. The term calculated is tantamount to words like computed, analyzed, and estimated. It suggests that you can predict the outcome. The reality is that when we are walking by faith and not by sight, we truly can predict that the outcome will be victorious in Christ.

We are told "Many are the plans in a person's heart, but it is the LORD'S PURPOSE THAT PREVAILS" (PROV. 19:21). Planning is important to God; it is encouraged by God. The outcome, however, is determined by God. Instead of saying it's a calculated risk, move forward with calculated faith. We can carefully estimate that the outcome will be for His glory and our good. Jesus said, "According to your faith let it be done to you" (Matt. 9:29). Amen!

## Prevailing in Planning

*Many are the plans in a person's heart, but it is the
LORD's purpose that prevails.*
*— Proverbs 19:21*

**Reflect on how you can prevail in this area of your life.**

---------------------------------------------------------------

---------------------------------------------------------------

---------------------------------------------------------------

---------------------------------------------------------------

---------------------------------------------------------------

---------------------------------------------------------------

---------------------------------------------------------------

---------------------------------------------------------------

---------------------------------------------------------------

---------------------------------------------------------------

---------------------------------------------------------------

Prayer: Precious Father in Heaven, I can trust You with my future and all the uncertainty that it holds. Whatever path You lead me to take, I know that You have gone before me to prepare the way. God, if it is viewed in the natural as a risk, then I trust that there is great reward. According to my faith, I believe You for the best outcome, in Jesus's name. Amen.

**I am prevailing in planning by faith,
in Jesus's name. Amen!**

## Scriptural Reference: 1 John 1:6-7

*If we claim to have fellowship with him and yet walk in
the darkness, we lie and do not live out the truth. But if we
walk in the light, as he is in the light, we have fellowship
with one another, and the blood of Jesus,
his Son, purifies us from all sin.*

# WALKING IN DARKNESS

For context, I have a walk-in closet with really high ceilings that used to have a motion light that only came on when I walked in it. Well, the fluorescent lights blew out, and we were not able to fix it on our own for several reasons. For starters, we did not have a ladder tall enough. Then, we discovered that it required wiring that my husband was unable to do. Because of our crazy schedules, we did not fix it quickly. You may find this funny, but I used a flash light for almost two months. I know that is absolutely crazy, but I did. Some days, I would walk in the closet without any lights at all, because I knew where I kept things. Eventually, it became extremely annoying. By the time I had the lights fixed, I had grown accustomed to walking in the dark. Once it was fixed, I no longer had the motion light and had to adjust to flipping the switch, which was not easy. One evening, my husband reminded me that I had lights now. As much as I had lamented about not having light in my closet, I was still comfortable walking in the dark. I realized that there was a message in this process.

Before we come into the saving knowledge of Jesus Christ, we are all comfortable walking in darkness. However, the Lord never intended for us to be comfortable in dark spaces or places. He has called us into His marvelous light. First John 1:6–7 says, "If we claim to have fellowship with him and yet walk in the darkness, we lie and do not live out the truth. But if we walk in the light, as he is in the light, we have fellowship with one another, and the blood of Jesus, his Son, purifies us from all sin." If we are believers in Jesus Christ, we have fellowship with the Savior and Redeemer of the world. Therefore, Jesus makes our way clear. Not only does He make our way clear, but He calls us to be "salt and light" in the earth (Matt. 5:13–14). We get the awesome privilege to represent the character of Jesus to the rest of the world. "For God, who said, 'Let light shine out of darkness,' made his light shine in our hearts to give us the light of the knowledge of God's glory displayed in the face of Christ" (2 Cor. 4:6).

## Prevailing over Darkness

*If we claim to have fellowship with him and yet walk in the darkness, we lie and do not live out the truth. But if we walk in the light, as he is in the light, we have fellowship with one another, and the blood of Jesus, his Son, purifies us from all sin.*
*— 1 John 1:6–7*

**Reflect on how you can prevail in this area of your life.**

_____

_____

_____

_____

_____

_____

_____

_____

_____

_____

_____

_____

_____

Prayer: God, thank You that You sent Jesus to be the light of the world and that whoever follows Him will not walk in darkness. I rejoice in the fact that I get to experience His marvelous light in my life. Amen!

**I am prevailing by being a light in dark places,
in Jesus's name. Amen!**

## Scriptural Reference: Hebrews 12:1-2

*Therefore, since we are surrounded by such a great cloud of witnesses, let us throw off everything that hinders and the sin that so easily entangles. And let us run with perseverance the race marked out for us, fixing our eyes on Jesus, the pioneer and perfecter of faith. For the joy set before him he endured the cross, scorning its shame, and sat down at the right hand of the throne of God.*

# WEIGHT LOSS

S ome years ago, a dear friend went to Europe during late February and early March. She talked about preparing for the anticipated cold weather there. She bought a heavy coat and sewed pockets and compartments inside of it to keep her personal items safe, including her passport and money. As she described it, the coat was very heavy to carry on her body every day; she felt weighed down. After leaving Europe and arriving back in the United States, she took the coat off and left it for someone to find. I knew how she felt after taking a similar trip to Europe during that same time of year. I wore a heavy coat along with multiple layers of clothing every day. It was exhausting to carry around and a relief to take it all off when I got inside. It's like that when you are physically carrying excess weight and you finally start shedding the pounds.

You also feel relief when you release your heavy burdens to the Lord. Ladies, ask yourself these questions: "What's weighing you down?" "What type of 'weight' do you need to lose?" Do not be confused and limit the scope of this question to shedding pounds, although the Lord may be dealing with you about that too. Think about deeper issues such as problems, fears, family, conflicts, sickness, finances, unforgiveness, anger, bitterness, discouragement, sadness, etc. We are commanded in God's word to strip "off everything that hinders ... run with perseverance the race marked out for us,

fixing our eyes on Jesus, the pioneer and perfecter of faith..."
(Heb. 12:1–2).

Any burden you are carrying instead of giving it to God
and allowing Him to make your burdens light, is excess
weight. Any circumstance or situation that you are trying
to solve on your own instead of trusting the Lord, you need
to lose that weight. Cast your cares on the LORD and he will
sustain you; he will never let the righteous be shaken" (Ps.
55:22). Amen!

## Prevailing in Weight Loss

*Therefore, since we are surrounded by such a great cloud of witnesses, let us throw off everything that hinders and the sin that so easily entangles. And let us run with perseverance the race marked out for us, fixing our eyes on Jesus, the pioneer and perfecter of faith. For the joy set before him he endured the cross, scorning its shame, and sat down at the right hand of the throne of God.*
*– Hebrews 12:1–2*

**Reflect on how you can prevail in this area of your life.**

_____

_____

_____

_____

_____

_____

_____

_____

_____

Prayer: Father God, I am throwing off every burden that is weighing me down and leaving them at the feet of Jesus. I am casting my cares, fears, anxieties, dreams, and problems for You to make them all light in my life. I thank You in advance for shedding these burdens. Amen.

**I am prevailing against carrying "weight" God did not intend me to carry, in Jesus's name. Amen!**

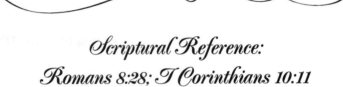

## Scriptural Reference:
## Romans 8:28; I Corinthians 10:11

*And we know that in all things God works for the good of those who love him, who have been called according to his purpose.*
*(Rom. 8:28)*

*These things happened to them as examples and were written down as warnings for us, on whom the culmination of the ages has come.*
*(1 Cor. 10:11)*

# GOD NEVER WASTES
# AN EXPERIENCE

My mother really wanted to protect me from making the same mistakes she made, and most of the time, I rebelled against her and was often disobedient. Saying, "Because I said so" was not a sufficient answer to why I could not do some of what I wanted to do. In my rebellion and disobedience, I had to experience some things for myself. Consequently, I made a lot of mistakes and experienced pains and disappointments or was exposed to things I could have avoided. Nevertheless, even in this, God never wastes an experience.

A similar message is recounted in this passage of scripture where Paul says, "These things happened to them as examples and were written down as warnings for us, on whom the culmination of the ages has come" (1 Cor. 10:11). Paul is reminding the Corinthians to avoid the mistakes of the Israelites pretty much the same way many of our parents tried to do to us when we were growing up. Perhaps that's your story. Perhaps you have had bad experiences that have shaped your life, and you learned the hard way instead of God's way, like me. However, every time I share an experience with someone, it is always a blessing and a source of encouragement. Several women that I know have bravely and courageously shared their experiences as testimonies to God's grace and deliverance, and invariably, someone always approached them afterward saying that they identified with their story.

Mistakes we have made and pains we have experienced are never without purpose. The fact that we lived through it all is a testimony. Our testimony could be a warning and can certainly be used to correct, rebuke, or instruct someone else. In retrospect, there are certainly some things I would have preferred not to have experienced. I also wish that I had listened to my mother more. We all have a story to tell, and we are each uniquely equipped to share our experiences to keep someone else from making the same mistakes. "And we know that in all things God works for the good of those who love him, who have been called according to his purpose" (Rom. 8:28). No experience is ever wasted; we just have to discern how God wants to use those experiences to help others. What can others learn from you?

## Prevailing in Not Wasting My Experiences

*These things happened to them as examples and were written down as warnings for us, on whom the culmination of the ages has come.* — 1 Corinthians 10:11

**Reflect on how you can prevail in this area of your life.**

_____

_____

_____

_____

_____

_____

_____

_____

_____

_____

_____

Prayer: Lord God, thank You that You cause all things to work together for my good and Your glory. I am grateful to You Lord that no experience is without purpose. I have numerous testimonies to share with others that will serve as wisdom and knowledge. Praise You Jesus for my life. Amen.

**I am prevailing in using my experiences for God's glory, in Jesus's name. Amen!**

## Scriptural Reference: Luke 6:27-28

*But to you who are listening I say: Love your enemies, do good to those who hate you, bless those who curse you, pray for those who mistreat you.*

# DISPLAYING GRACE TO YOUR ENEMY

G race is defined as unmerited favor shown to someone who does not deserve it. Sometimes that "someone" is your enemy. A person is considered your enemy when their whole purpose is to destroy you, berate you, impugn your integrity, speak negatively about you, and perhaps to you. An enemy is clearly not your friend but only a negative force designed to be problematic in your life. I have at one point been someone's enemy, and at other times, I may have been perceived as an enemy when there was no basis for it. I have also had my share of enemies, and even today, there are people I would classify as an enemy. Admittedly, I am still maturing in this area. I have been put in a situation where I had to display grace to someone I perceived to be an enemy. (As a side note: You can have enemies within your own family.)

I willfully and intentionally avoid known and perceived enemies just to protect myself from being hurt by their words or actions. I have been impressed with how I have seen other people show grace to known enemies. I was in awe watching a colleague who was unjustly misrepresented and inappropriately bashed in a newspaper meet with the individual who wrote those things. In addition, they gave the person a captive audience in which to speak. It was a lesson for me and others who knew about the incident. Despite all of that, it was clear that grace was extended in order to maintain honor, great leadership, dignity, and decorum. Don't get me wrong, I have forgiven many people for pain they've caused me, but I just don't want to hang out with them. Jesus said, "But to you who are listening I say: Love your enemies, do good to those who hate you" (Lk. 6:27). We are commanded to seek the best and do good for our enemies. Whew! That is true unconditional love on display. Only by God's grace are we able to practice what Jesus preached!

# Prevailing in Displaying Grace to our Enemies

*But to you who are listening I say: Love your enemies,*
*do good to those who hate you.*
*— Luke 6:27*

—⁂—

## Reflect on how you can prevail in this area of your life.

_____

_____

_____

_____

_____

_____

_____

_____

_____

_____

_____

_____

Dear Heavenly Father, I acknowledge that it is difficult to display Your grace to people who are considered an enemy. Please empower me with Your spirit to extend Your amazing grace to persons perceived as enemies. Shield and protect me as I emulate You to them.

**I am prevailing in displaying grace to my enemies,
in Jesus's name. Amen!**

## *Scriptural Reference: Matthew 9: 20-22*

*Just then a woman who had been subject to bleeding for twelve years came up behind him and touched the edge of his cloak. She said to herself, "If I only touch his cloak, I will be healed." Jesus turned and saw her. "Take heart, daughter," he said, "your faith has healed you." And the woman was healed at that moment.*

# HE IS A MIRACLE WORKER

L ike so many believers, I have had the awesome privilege of seeing God perform miracles and blessings in the lives of family and friends. Imagine being diagnosed with a brain tumor and not being sure how the doctors would remove it from behind your eye and then having a procedure performed to shrink it. That is the testimony of my mother. My cousin was faced with a life-altering decision when she was four months pregnant. She was forced to choose between her baby's life and her own because she was diagnosed with stage four breast cancer. Imagine the doctor telling you they could give you chemotherapy during your pregnancy, and you still deliver a healthy baby. Imagine being sick with a terminal illness for fourteen years, yet you are still alive while many close to you have died. That is the testimony of a dear friend and so many others. All these women, whom I personally know, are alive today by God's grace. God is a miracle worker. Ladies, we have some walking, living, breathing miracles among us.

God is a healer and a sustainer. There is no way to explain these acts other than His miraculous hand being upon each of these individuals lives. But they are not the first miracles. God has been performing miracles all throughout history. I am reminded of the woman with the issue of blood.

The woman with the issue of blood was healed at the moment she demonstrated great faith. This woman pressed her way through every obstacle to get to Jesus. She didn't let any doctors report keep her from pursuing her healing. She didn't let naysayers cloud her judgment or serve as discouragement. She didn't even mind getting dirty to get cleaned as she was basically on the ground reaching for the hem of Jesus's garment. She focused only on her desired outcome, which was to be healed by Jesus. She firmly believed without doubting that if she got to Jesus, He would do it according to her faith. She is the epitome of a prevailing woman. She was focused, had a plan, was unwavering in her pursuit, had faith and trust in God, and did not allow anything to stand in the way of her destiny. Use this woman as an example to you pursuing your purpose, whether you need physical or spiritual healing, or just a breakthrough in some other area or situation of your life.

Prevailing woman, my prayer for you comes in this scripture, "Dear friend, I pray that you may enjoy good health and that all may go well with you, even as your soul is getting along well" (3 Jn. 1:2).

# Prevailing in Believing God

*Just then a woman who had been subject to bleeding for twelve years came up behind him and touched the edge of his cloak. She said to herself, "If I only touch his cloak, I will be healed." Jesus turned and saw her. "Take heart, daughter," he said, "your faith has healed you." And the woman was healed at that moment.*
*— Matthew 9:20–22*

**Reflect on how you can prevail in this area of your life.**

_____

_____

_____

_____

_____

_____

_____

Holy Father, You are too wonderful for words. How I magnify You for Your marvelous and miraculous works in the earth and throughout scripture. God, I believe You for healing in my life and in the lives of those connected to me. What is impossible with man, is possible with You, Lord God. As You show Yourself faithful to be a healer and sustainer, I will be careful to give Your name the praise and honor it is due. In the matchless name of Jesus, the Christ, amen.

**I am prevailing in believing God for miracles,**
**in Jesus's name. Amen!**

## Scriptural Reference:
## John 4:4-7,9-10, 13-15, 28-29

*Now he had to go through Samaria. So he came to a town in Samaria called Sychar, near the plot of ground Jacob had given to his son Joseph. Jacob's well was there, and Jesus, tired as he was from the journey, sat down by the well. It was about noon. When a Samaritan woman came to draw water, Jesus said to her, "Will you give me a drink?" ...The Samaritan woman said to him, "You are a Jew and I am a Samaritan woman. How can you ask me for a drink?" (For Jews do not associate with Samaritans.) Jesus answered her, "If you knew the gift of God and who it is that asks you for a drink, you would have asked him and he would have given you living water."...Jesus answered, "Everyone who drinks this water will be thirsty again, but whoever drinks the water I give them will never thirst. Indeed, the water I give them will become in them a spring of water welling up to eternal life." The woman said to him, "Sir, give me this water so that I won't get thirsty and have to keep coming here to draw water." ...Then, leaving her water jar, the woman went back to the town and said to the people, "Come, see a man who told me everything I ever did. Could this be the Messiah?"*

# EVERYTHING I EVER DID

The Samaritan woman in John 4 had an encounter that she could not contain. In this chapter, Jesus made an interesting (yet purposeful) decision. He determined that it was necessary for Him to go through Samaria. To understand the significance of this decision, customarily Samaritans and Jews didn't have anything to do with each other. So, Jesus detours intentionally to have a divine encounter with a woman who quickly became one of the most compelling witnesses to the transforming power of Jesus.

Have you ever looked at someone's life and thought to yourself, *how in the world did they ever make a change?* Then answered yourself saying, *If God can change them, He can change anyone.* I think about my own life before I met Jesus and even afterward. Knowing my life's story, it would not be desirable to meet someone who could tell me everything that I ever did. If you are like me, you don't want anyone to tell you about everything you have done. The Samaritan woman was living a sinful lifestyle, specifically by cohabitating with men she was not married to. The behavior violated all biblical standards and customs of that time, and it still does today, even though we have become more acceptable of certain societal norms.

The Samaritan woman was called out by Jesus, not just for the man she was currently living with, but also for five other men who were not her husband either. She was very aware of her lifestyle being perceived as unacceptable. In fact, she carried that shame every day. She didn't socialize with other women who drew water from that same well. In fact, she avoided them because she drew her water during the middle of the day when she knew no other woman would be present. Take a mental note here: the enemy uses shame and secrecy as a tactic to separate us from opportunities to be set free. Her primary interaction was with men who did not belong to her. She had no normal social interaction with other women.

For this Samaritan woman to have gone from one man to the next, she had to have not seen a way out of her situation until she met Jesus at the well. In fact, until anyone meets Jesus, they have no way out.

If you are reading this and are in a situation where you don't see a way out, hear this, God is your way out. Perhaps you are concerned that your lifestyle and choices disqualify you from ever experiencing God's redemption. Maybe you live in a place where everybody knows what you used to do, and you think you will be judged. Jesus waits at the well for you too! Don't let the fear of what others might say keep you from drinking from the Living Water of Jesus. He will keep you from thirsting again for the same old lifestyle.

The truth set the Samaritan woman free. Then, she immediately started sharing with others. The woman left her lifestyle once she met the Messiah and then exclaimed with freedom and gladness, "Come, see a man who told me everything I ever did..." (Jn. 4:29).

## Prevailing over Everything I Ever Did

*Jesus answered her, "If you knew the gift of God and who it
is that asks you for a drink, you would have asked him and
he would have given you living water."...Jesus answered,
"Everyone who drinks this water will be thirsty again, but
whoever drinks the water I give them will never thirst...Come,
see a man who told me everything I ever did...*
*— John 4:10, 13, 29*

**Reflect on how you can prevail in this area of your life.**

_____

_____

_____

_____

_____

_____

_____

_____

Father God, how grateful I am that You are the ONLY one
who knows everything I have ever done and yet still loves
me. Thank you, Lord God, for being Living Water for me.
You have poured out Your love, grace, and mercy on my life.
You sent Jesus to meet me at "my well" and for this reason
I am free today. I praise You for my redemption, restoration,
and the revelation of knowing what You have done for me.

**I am prevailing over every bad decision I have ever made,
in Jesus's name. Amen!**

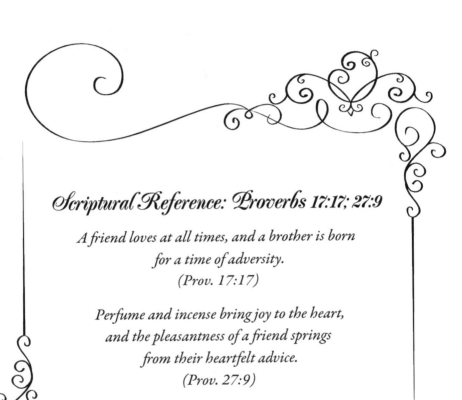

## Scriptural Reference: Proverbs 17:17; 27:9

*A friend loves at all times, and a brother is born*
*for a time of adversity.*
*(Prov. 17:17)*

*Perfume and incense bring joy to the heart,*
*and the pleasantness of a friend springs*
*from their heartfelt advice.*
*(Prov. 27:9)*

# FRIENDSHIP

As I write this, the lines to a rap song by the group Whodini started ringing in my head. Those of you who know the song "Friends" will be singing it too. The song asks what I believe to be a rhetorical question about how many of us have friends we can depend on. Over the years, I have acquired and developed an array of friendships. Some of those relationships were seasonal, but most of them have been for a lifetime. As I have gotten older, I am more intentional about my relationships. I value them more and have some regrets about some relationships that grew distant due to life transitions. I find myself now being incredibly grateful for the beautiful women the Lord has surrounded me with over the years.

What I have come to realize is that a prevailing woman needs to be surrounded and connected with other prevailing women. Praise be to God, I am! One friend asked me how I kept up with my relationships and wondered if I talked to everyone often. Admittedly, I do talk to some of my friends more than others, but as soon as I connect with others, it's as if we spoke just the day before. I have some ride or die kind of friends. I have sisters! I have women who hold me accountable. They speak wisdom and give me wise counsel. They encourage me. My friends have made and continue to make me better. They sharpen me as described in scripture: "As iron sharpens iron, so one person sharpens another" (Prov. 27:17).

I am the only girl, and the oldest out of my three brothers. God blessed me to have sisters through my friends, some of my cousins, and one of my aunts. My friendships outside of family members have brought me enormous joy. I write this to say that I wish this type of relationship for every woman on the face of the earth. Ladies, we need relationships that build us up, hold us accountable, correct us, rebuke us, help us, sacrifice for us, and simply love us in all our imperfections. The Bible says, "A friend loves at all times, and a brother is born for a time of adversity" (Prov. 17:17). Develop authentic relationships with women that make it safe to "keep it real." In Christ, we have a friend in Jesus. While there is no substitute for the relationship we have with Jesus Christ, our earthly relationships should reflect the love of Christ. I am immeasurably blessed by my relationships and for those who have intimately walked alongside me during some of my darkest and most difficult days. My prayer is that wherever you are in life, that God will bless you with another prevailing woman or a whole group of prevailing women who can pour into your life, and you can, in return, pour into them. Be a great friend to get a great friend. To God be the glory for the prevailing women in my life! I love you all.

# Prevailing in Friendships

*Perfume and incense bring joy to the heart, and the pleasantness of a friend springs from their heartfelt advice.* — Proverbs 27:9

**Reflect on how you can prevail in this area of your life.**

Prayer: Holy Father, I praise You for the godly friends You have put in my life. I pray that every woman connects with women who will be a blessing and source of encouragement to them. May I be a good friend to all the people with whom I am blessed to build a relationship. Amen.

**I am prevailing in being a godly friend,
in Jesus's name. Amen!**

# BIBLIOGRAPHY

1. Amplified Bible, The Lockman Foundation, (La Habra, CA, 90631, 2015).

2. Webster's Ninth New Collegiate Dictionary, (Springfield, Massachusetts, 1988).

3. Holy Bible, New International Version.

# ABOUT THE AUTHOR

D r. Samantha W. Murfree is best described as a teacher, speaker, exhorter, and communicator of God's Word. She infuses her life experiences through her teachings, including the good, bad, ugly, and painful, along with her struggles and joys, as a testimony to God's goodness, mercy, and grace. She is an example of how God's redemptive power healed, delivered, and set her free from the chains that had her bound.

Samantha is a native Mississippian, born in Jackson. Her family primarily resided in the small town of Georgetown. She grew up attending New Hope Missionary Baptist Church, where her spiritual foundation was established by attending Sunday school.

She attended Tougaloo College, a private historically black college and university (HBCU) in MS, and the University of Missouri-Columbia, where she received her Bachelor of Arts in Psychology and Master of Arts degree in Educational and Counseling Psychology, respectively. After several years working as a student-affairs professional, she went back to school at the University of Georgia to obtain her Doctor of Philosophy (PhD) in Counseling and Student Personnel Services, with an emphasis in Student Affairs Administration and Higher Education. She obtained credentialing as a Licensed Professional Counselor and National Certified Counselor. Though she is no longer active as a professional counselor, she maintains credentialing as a retired

131

National Certified Counselor. Currently, Dr. Murfree has over twenty years of higher education experience. Most recently, Dr. Murfree founded and established Prevailing Woman Ministries, Inc., for which she serves as its executive director.

As Dr. Murfree's career led her to live in various locations, it was also a way for her to grow and mature in her relationship with the Lord Jesus Christ. She grew through opportunities to serve. She taught and directed Vacation Bible School, led small-group Bible studies for women, engaged in Single's Ministry when she was single, participated in the church visitation ministry, choir/praise team, Marriage and Relationship Ministry, New Members Ministry (and currently serves as the group's director at her church, Beulahland Bible Church), and was certified in Evangelism Explosion. All these experiences and much more served to shape Samantha's calling and purpose.

Samantha married Dr. Joshua W. Murfree Jr. in 2009. The Murfrees make room in their busy lives to pour into the lives of others as opportunities are presented. Samantha's passion is connecting with women and serving as an encouragement to them.

CPSIA information can be obtained
at www.ICGtesting.com
Printed in the USA
FFHW01n1930260918